American Mathematics Competitions 8 Practice

http://www.mymathcounts.com/index.php

This book can be used by students who are preparing for middle school math competitions such as American Mathematics Competitions 8, Mathcounts, or SAT I and II math exams.

Some of the problems in this book were modified from or inspired by 2000–2010 American Mathematics Competitions 8. Some of the problems were written by the author. All solutions were written by the author.

Please contact mymathcounts@gmail.com for suggestions, corrections, or clarifications.

Contributors

Yongcheng Chen, Ph.D., Author.
Guiling Chen, Owner, mymathcounts.com, Typesetter, Editor

© 2013 mymathcounts.com. All rights reserved. Printed in the United States of America Reproduction of any portion of this book without the written permission of the authors is strictly prohibited, except as may be expressly permitted by the U.S. Copyright Act.

ISBN-13: 978-1493582259
ISBN-10: 1493582259

Table of Contents

1. American Mathematics Competitions 8 Practice test 1 and solutions   1

2. American Mathematics Competitions 8 Practice test 2 and solutions   15

3. American Mathematics Competitions 8 Practice test 3 and solutions   28

4. American Mathematics Competitions 8 Practice test 4 and solutions   40

5. American Mathematics Competitions 8 Practice test 5 and solutions   53

6. American Mathematics Competitions 8 Practice test 6 and solutions   66

7. American Mathematics Competitions 8 Practice test 7 and solutions   77

8. American Mathematics Competitions 8 Practice test 8 and solutions   89

9. American Mathematics Competitions 8 Practice test 9 and solutions   102

10. American Mathematics Competitions 8 Practice test 10 and solutions   117

Index   127

This page is intentionally left blank.

American Mathematics Competitions

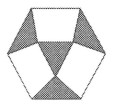

Practice 1
AMC 8
(American Mathematics Contest 8)

INSTRUCTIONS

1. DO NOT OPEN THIS BOOKLET UNTIL YOUR PROCTOR TELLS YOU.

2. This is a twenty-five question multiple choice test. Each question is followed by answers marked A, B, C, D and E. Only one of these is correct.

3. Mark your answer to each problem on the AMC 8 Answer Form with a #2 pencil. Check the blackened circles for accuracy and erase errors and stray marks completely. Only answers properly marked on the answer form will be graded.

4. There is no penalty for guessing. Your score on this test is the number of correct answers.

5. No aids are permitted other than scratch paper, graph paper, rulers, and erasers. No problems on the test will require the use of a calculator.

6. Figures are not necessarily drawn to scale.

7. Before beginning the test, your proctor will ask you to record certain information on the answer form.

8. When your proctor gives the signal, begin working on the problems. You will have 40 minutes to complete the test.

9. When you finish the exam, *sign your name* in the space provided on the Answer Form.

American Math Competition 8 Practice   Test 1

1. Alex had $20 to spend at the carnival. He spent $4 on food and twice as much on rides. How many dollars did he have left to spend?
(A) 12   (B) 8   (C) 6   (D) 16   (E) 14

2. The nine-letter code MATHISFUN represents the nine digits 1–9, in order. What 4-digit number is represented by the code word FISH?
(A) 7564   (B) 7654   (C) 75654   (D) 9782   (E) 9872

3. If September is a month that contains Friday the 13th, what day of the week is September 1?
(A) Sunday (B) Monday (C) Wednesday (D) Thursday (E) Saturday

4. In the figure, the outer square has area 48, the inner square has area 24, and the four triangles are congruent. What is the area of one of the triangles?
(A) 12   (B) 15   (C) 6   (D) 10   (E) 7

5. Bob notices that the odometer on his bicycle reads 141, a palindrome, because it reads the same forward and backward. After riding 4 more hours that day, he notices that the odometer shows another palindrome, 161. What was his average speed in miles per hour?
(A) 15   (B) 6   (C) 8   (D) 4   (E) 5

6. As shown in the figure, ABC is an equilateral triangle. Each dot is the midpoint of the corresponding line segment. Find the ratio of the area of the gray rhombus to the area of the white triangles?
(A) 2 : 7   (B) 3 : 16   (C) 3 : 15   (D) 1 : 7   (E) 1 : 5

7. If $\frac{5}{7} = \frac{x}{56} = \frac{y}{14}$, what is $x + y$?

(A) 40   (B) 29   (C) 45   (D) 70   (E) 50

8. Candy sales of the Math Club for January through April are shown. Find the average sales per month in dollars.

(A) 75   (B) 125   (C) 75   (D) 100   (E) 85

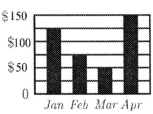

9. In 2010 Betsy invested $1000 for two years. During the first year her investment suffered a 10% loss, but during the second year the remaining investment showed a 10% gain. Over the two-year period, what was the change in Betsy's investment?

(A) 2% gain gain   (B) 2% loss   (C) 1% gain   (D) 1% loss   (E) neither loss nor gain

10. The average age of the 12 people in Room A is 12. The average age of the 8 people in Room B is 7. If the two groups are combined, what is the average age of all the people?

(A) 9.5   (B) 8   (C) 11.2   (D) 10   (E) 11

11. Each of the 100 students in the eighth grade at Hope Middle School has one dog or one cat or both a dog and a cat. Seventy-three students have a dog and 90 students have a cat. How many students have a cat but not a dog?

(A) 27   (B) 63   (C) 73   (D) 69   (E) 46

12. A ball is dropped from a height of 9 meters. On its first bounce it rises to a height of 6 meters. It keeps falling and bouncing to 2/3 of the height it reached in the previous bounce. On which bounce will it not rise to a height of 1.5 meters?

(A) 3   (B) 4   (C) 5   (D) 6   (E) 7

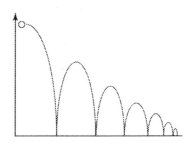

13. Mr. Harman needs to know the combined weight in pounds of four boxes he wants to mail. However, the only available scale is not accurate for weights less than 20 pounds or more than 30 pounds. So the boxes are weighed in triples in every possible way. The results are 21, 28, 29, and 30 pounds. What is the possible sum of the weight in pounds of the two boxes?

(A) 12 (B) 24 (C) 21 (D) 19 (E) 13

14. Three As, three Bs and three Cs are placed in the nine spaces so that each row and column contain one of each letter. If A is placed in the middle as shown, how many arrangements are possible?

(A) 2 (B) 3 (C) 4 (D) 5 (E) 6

15. In Lisa's first 8 basketball games, she scored 7, 4, 7, 6, 8, 3, 8 and 5 points. In her ninth game, she scored fewer than 10 points and her points-per-game average for the nine games was an integer. Similarly in her tenth game, she scored fewer than 10 points and her points-per-game average for the 10 games was also an integer. Find the product of the number of points she scored in the ninth and tenth games.

(A) 35 (B) 36 (C) 48 (D) 56 (E) 40

American Math Competition 8 Practice — Test 1

16. A shape is created by joining seven unit cubes, as shown. What is the ratio of the perimeter of the solid in units to the surface area in square units?
(A) 6 : 1   (B) 7 : 1   (C) 5 : 1   (D) 2 : 1   (E) 25 : 6

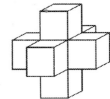

17. A rectangle with integer side lengths has a perimeter of 60 units. Find the difference between the largest and smallest possible areas of the rectangle.
(A) 76   (B) 120   (C) 128   (D) 196   (E) 136

18. Two circles that share the same center have radii 10 meters and 20 meters. Alex runs along the path shown, starting at A, passing through K, and ending at A. How many meters does Alex run?
(A) $10\pi + 20$ (B) $10\pi + 30$ (C) $10\pi + 40$
(D) $20\pi + 20$ (E) $25\pi + 60$

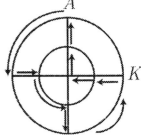

19. Nine points are spaced at intervals of one unit around a 2×2 square, as shown. Two of the 9 points are chosen at random. What is the probability that the points are one unit apart?
(A) 1/4   (B) 1/3   (C) 2/7   (D) 1/2   (E) 4/7

20. The students in Mr. Chen's math club took a penmanship test. Three-seventh of the boys and 8/11 of the girls passed the test, and an equal number of boys and girls passed the test. What is the minimum possible number of students in the class?
(A) 72   (B) 89   (C) 84   (D) 56   (E) 33

American Math Competition 8 Practice   Test 1

21. Jerry cuts a wedge from a 6-cm cylinder of bologna as shown by the dashed curve. Which answer choice is closest to the volume of his wedge in cubic centimeters?
 (A) 25π (B) 75π (C) 90π (D) 144π (E) 603

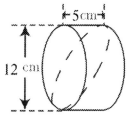

22. Find the number of positive integer values of n such that $n/7$ is a three-digit whole number and $7n$ a four-digit whole number.
 (A) 105 (B) 121 (C) 127 (D) 133 (E) 34

23. In rectangle $ABCE$, $AF = 3FE$ and $ED = 4DC$. What is the ratio of the area of $\triangle BFD$ to the area of square $ABCE$?
 (A) 1/6 (B) 2/9 (C) 17/40 (D) 1/3
 (E) 17/20

24. Alex selects a positive integer less than 11, and Bob selects a positive integer less than 14. What is the probability that the product of the two numbers selected will be a square number?
 (A) 1/10 (B) 17/108 (C) 19/130 (D) 3/22 (E) 17/154

25. As shown in the figure, the smallest circle has radius 5 inches, with each successive circle's radius increasing by 5 inches. What is the probability that a dart thrown at random will land in the white area?
 (A) 7/12 (B) 43/100 (C) 5/11 (D) 4/13 (E) 21/100

American Math Competition 8 Practice   Test 1

SOLUTIONS

1. Solution (B): Alex spent $2 \times 4 = \$8$ on rides, so she had $20 - 4 - 8 = \$8$ to spend.

2. Solution (A): Because the key to the code starts with zero, all the letters represent numbers that are one less than their position

M	A	T	H	I	S	F	U	N
1	2	3	4	5	6	7	8	9

FISH = 7564

3. Solution (A): A week before the 13th is the 6th, which is the first Friday of the month. Counting back from that, the 5th is a Thursday, the 4th is a Wednesday, the 3rd is a Tuesday, the 2nd is a Monday, and the 1st is a Sunday.

4. Solution (C): The area of the outer triangle with the inner triangle removed is $48 - 24 = 24$, the total area of the four congruent triangles. Each triangle has area $24/4 = 6$.

5. Solution (E): Barney rides $161 - 141 = 20$ miles in 4 hours, so his average speed is $20/4 = 5$ miles per hour.

6. Solution (D): After subdividing the figure as shown, 2 of the 16 congruent triangles are gray and 14 are white. Therefore, the ratio of the area of the gray rhombus to the area of the white triangles is $2 : 14$ or $1 : 7$.

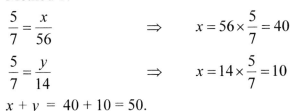

7. Solution (E):
Method 1:
$$\frac{5}{7} = \frac{x}{56} \quad \Rightarrow \quad x = 56 \times \frac{5}{7} = 40$$
$$\frac{5}{7} = \frac{y}{14} \quad \Rightarrow \quad x = 14 \times \frac{5}{7} = 10$$
$x + y = 40 + 10 = 50$.

Method 2:

American Math Competition 8 Practice — Test 1

$$\frac{5}{7} = \frac{x}{56} = \frac{y}{14} = \frac{x+y}{56+14} \quad \Rightarrow \quad x+y = 70 \times \frac{5}{7} = 50.$$

8. Solution (D): The sales in the 4 months were $125, $75, $50 and $150. The average sales were (125 + 75 + 50 + 150)/4 = $100.

9. Solution (D): At the end of the first year, Betsy's investment was 90% of the original amount, or $900. At the end of the second year, she had 100% of her first year's final amount, or 110% of $900 = 1.1($900) = $990. Over the two-year period, Betsy's investment changed from $1000 to $990, so she had (1000 − 990) / 1000 = 1% loss.

Or $0.9 \times 1.1 = 0.99$. so she had (1 − 0.99) = 1% loss.

10. Solution (D): The sum of the ages of the 12 people in Room A is 12 × 12 = 144. The sum of the ages of the 8 people in Room B is 8 × 7 = 56. The sum of the ages of the 20 people in the combined group is 144 + 56 = 200, so the average age of all the people is 200/20 = 10.

11. Solution: 27 (students).
The question wants us to find the number of students have a cat but not a dog.
This is the same as finding the number of elementary in Set B only.
Set A: number of students having a dog (73).
Set B: number of students having a cat (90).
Intersection of A and B can be calculated by $n(A \cup B) = n(A) + n(B) - n(A \cap B)$.

$$n(A \cup B) = n(A) + n(B) - n(A \cap B)$$
$$\uparrow \qquad \uparrow \qquad \uparrow$$
$$\text{Known} \quad \text{Known} \quad \text{Unknown}$$

$100 = 73 + 90 - n(A \cap B) \quad \Rightarrow \quad n(A \cap B) = 63.$

We have two ways to calculate the number of students having a dog only: 100 − 73 = 27 or 90 − 63 = 27.
The Venn diagram is as follows:

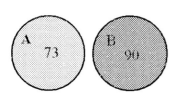 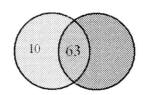

12. Solution (C): The table gives the height of each bounce.

Bounce	1	2	3	4	5
Height	$9 \times \frac{2}{3}$	$9 \times (\frac{2}{3})^2$	$9 \times (\frac{2}{3})^3$	$9 \times (\frac{2}{3})^4 = \frac{16}{9} = 1.\overline{7}$	$9 \times (\frac{2}{3})^5 = \frac{32}{27} < \frac{3}{2} = 1.5$

13. Solution (C):
Let the sum of these four numbers be x. the four numbers then are: $x - 21$, $x - 28$, $x - 29$, and $x - 30$.
$(x - 21) + (x - 28) + (x - 29) + (x - 30) = x \quad \Rightarrow \quad x = 36$.
$x - 21 = 36 - 21 = 15$.
$x - 28 = 36 - 28 = 8$.
$x - 29 = 36 - 29 = 7$.
$x - 30 = 36 - 30 = 6$.
So the answer is $15 + 6 = 21$.

14. Solution (C):
The As can be placed in two ways:

In each case, the letter next to the top A can be B or C. At that point the rest of the grid is completely determined. So there are $2 + 2 = 4$ possible arrangements.

15. Solution (B): The sum of the points Lisa scored in the first 8 games is 48. After the ninth game, her point total must be a multiple of 9 between 48 and 48 + 9 = 57, inclusive. The only such point total is 54 = 48 + 6, so in the ninth game she scored 6 points. Similarly, the next point total must be a multiple of 10 between 54 and 54 + 9 = 63. The only such point total is 60 = 54 + 6, so in the tenth game she scored 6 points. The product of the number of points scored in Lisa's ninth and tenth games is 6 × 6 = 36.

16. Solution (D):
There are 12 units of side lengths of each cube. 12 × 6 = 72. Each cube lost 4 sides when the cubes are put together. 6 × 4 = 24. The cube we could not see has the side length of 12 units. So the perimeter is 72 − 24 + 12 = 60.
We view the solid from top we see
We will see the same shape from bottom. There are six directions: front, back, top, bottom, left and right, for a total of 5 × 6 = 30 square units of surface area.

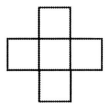

The ratio of the perimeter to the surface area is 60 : 30 = 2:1.

17. Solution (D): The formula for the perimeter of a rectangle is $2l + 2w$, so $2l + 2w = 60$, and $l + w = 30$. When $l + w$ is fixed, $l \times w$ will have the largest area if the difference of l and w is as small as possible. So let $l = w = 15$. The largest possible area is 15 × 15 = 225.

When $l + w$ is fixed, $l \times w$ will have the smallest area if the difference of l and w is as large as possible. The smallest area is 1 × 29 = 29.
The difference between the largest and smallest possible areas of the rectangle is 225 − 29 = 196 square units.

18. Solution (E):
Alex runs half of the large circle, a quarter of small circle, and 3 radii of the large circle.
The length is $\dfrac{2\pi \times 20}{2} + \dfrac{2\pi \times 10}{4} + 3 \times 20 = 25\pi + 60$ meters.

19. Solution (B):
Method 1:

We have $\binom{9}{2} = \frac{9 \times 8}{2} = 36$ possible pairs.

We have 12 segments 1 unit long. The probability is 12/36 = 1/3.

Method 2:
Case I: We first pick up the corner point:
The probability to pick up the corner point is 4/9. Figure (a).

Then we pick up the second point. The probability to pick up the point that is 1 unit from the first point is 2/8. Figure (b).

The profanity is $P_1 = \frac{4}{9} \times \frac{2}{8} = \frac{1}{9}$.

Figure (a)   Figure (b)

Case II: We first pick up the point as shown:
The probability to pick up that point is 4/9. Figure (c).
Then we pick up the second point. The probability to pick up the point that is 1 unit from the first point is 3/8. Figure (d).

The profanity is $P_2 = \frac{4}{9} \times \frac{3}{8} = \frac{1}{6}$.

Figure (c)   Figure (d)

Case III: We first pick up the center point as shown.
The probability to pick up the center point is 1/9. Figure (e).
Then we pick up the second point. The probability to pick up the point that is 1 unit from the first point is 4/8 = 1/2. Figure (f)

The profanity is $P_3 = \frac{1}{9} \times \frac{1}{2} = \frac{1}{18}$.

Figure (e)   Figure (f)

The answer is $P = \frac{1}{9} + \frac{1}{6} + \frac{1}{18} = \frac{2+3+1}{18} = \frac{6}{18} = \frac{1}{3}$.

20. Solution: (B).
Let G = the number of girls and B = the number of boys. Then
$\frac{3}{7}b = \frac{8}{11}g \quad \Rightarrow \quad 33b = 56g$

Because 33 and 56 are relatively prime, the minimum number of boys is 56 and the minimum number of girls is 33, for a total of 56 + 33 = 89 students.

21. Solution (C):
Using the formula for the volume of a cylinder, the bologna has volume
$V = \pi r^2 h = 6^2 \times 5\pi = 180\pi$

The cut divides the bologna in half. The half-cylinder will have volume 90π.

22. Solution (A):
Because $n/7$ is at least 100 and is an integer, n is at least 700 and is a multiple of 7.

Because $7n$ is at most 9999, n is at most 1428.

The possible values of n are 700, 707, ,..., 1428. This is an arithmetic sequence with $a_m = 1428$, $a_1 = 700$ and common difference 7.
So $1428 = 700 + (m - 1) \times 7 \quad \Rightarrow \quad m = 105$.

23. Solution: (C).

Method 1:

Let $AF = 3x$, $FE = x$, $ED = 4y$ and $DC = y$.

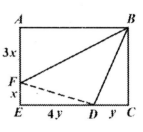

$S_{\triangle ABCE} = 4x \times 5y = 20xy$. $S_{\triangle ABF} = \dfrac{3x \times 5y}{2}$. $S_{\triangle BCD} = \dfrac{4x \times y}{2} = 2xy$.

$S_{\triangle EDF} = \dfrac{x \times 4y}{2} = 2xy$.

$S_{ABCD} = S_{\triangle BFD} + S_{\triangle ABF} + S_{\triangle BCD} + S_{\triangle EDF}$

$S_{\triangle BFD} = 20xy - 2xy - 2xy - \dfrac{15}{2}xy = \dfrac{17}{2}xy$

$\dfrac{S_{\triangle BFD}}{S_{\triangle ABCE}} = \dfrac{\frac{17}{2}xy}{20xy} = \dfrac{17}{40}$.

Method 2:

In rectangle $ABCD$, we have: $S_{ABCD} = 2S_{\triangle BFD} + AF \times DC$.

Then:

$\dfrac{2S_{\triangle BFD}}{S_{ABCD}} = 1 - \dfrac{AF \times DC}{S_{ABCD}} \quad \Rightarrow$

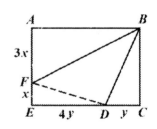

$\dfrac{S_{\triangle BFD}}{S_{ABCD}} = \dfrac{1}{2}(1 - \dfrac{AF \times DC}{S_{ABCD}}) = \dfrac{1}{2}(1 - \dfrac{3x \times y}{4x \times 5y}) = \dfrac{1}{2}(1 - \dfrac{3}{20}) = \dfrac{17}{40}$

24. Solution: (C). $\dfrac{19}{130}$.

There are $10 \times 13 = 130$ possible pairs. The squares less than 130 are 1, 4, 9, 16, 25, 36, 49 64, 81, 100, and 121. The possible pairs with products equal to the given squares are
(1, 1), (2, 2), (3, 3), (4, 4), (5, 5), (6, 6), (7, 7), (8, 8), (9, 9), (10, 10).
(1, 4), (4, 1), (1, 9), (9, 1), (2, 8), (8, 2), (4, 9), (9, 4), (3, 12).
So the probability is 19/130.

25. Solution: (A).

The areas are:

Circle 1: $\pi \times 5^2 = 25\pi$

Circle 1: $\pi \times 10^2 = 100\pi$

The area of the white area $A = 100\pi - 25\pi = 75\pi$

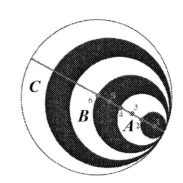

Circle 3: $\pi \times 15^2 = 225\pi$

Circle 4: $\pi \times 20^2 = 400\pi$

The area of the white area $B = 400\pi - 225\pi = 175\pi$

Circle 5: $\pi \times 25^2 = 625\pi$

Circle 6: $\pi \times 30^2 = 900\pi$

The area of the white area $C = 900\pi - 625\pi = 275\pi$.

The total area is 900π and the white area is $(275 + 175 + 75)\pi = 525\pi$. The answer is $525\pi/900\pi = 7/12$.

American Mathematics Competitions

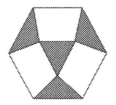

Practice 2
AMC 8

(American Mathematics Contest 8)

INSTRUCTIONS

1. DO NOT OPEN THIS BOOKLET UNTIL YOUR PROCTOR TELLS YOU.

2. This is a twenty-five question multiple choice test. Each question is followed by answers marked A, B, C, D and E. Only one of these is correct.

3. Mark your answer to each problem on the AMC 8 Answer Form with a #2 pencil. Check the blackened circles for accuracy and erase errors and stray marks completely. Only answers properly marked on the answer form will be graded.

4. There is no penalty for guessing. Your score on this test is the number of correct answers.

5. No aids are permitted other than scratch paper, graph paper, rulers, and erasers. No problems on the test will require the use of a calculator.

6. Figures are not necessarily drawn to scale.

7. Before beginning the test, your proctor will ask you to record certain information on the answer form.

8. When your proctor gives the signal, begin working on the problems. You will have 40 minutes to complete the test.

9. When you finish the exam, *sign your name* in the space provided on the Answer

American Math Competition 8 Practice   Test 2

1. In a factory, a machine can fill 8 jars in 3 minutes. How many minutes does it need to fill 24 jars?
(A) 6   (B) 623   (C) 712   (D) 8   (E) 9

2. Mother Chickadee brings in a worm every 3 hours and her baby bird eats 6 worms every day. To the nearest hundred, how many worms are stored by them each year?
(A) 600   (B) 700   (C) 800   (D) 900   (E) 1000

3. If it was 9:20 am 45 minutes ago, in how many minutes will it be noon?
(A) 125   (B) 115   (C) 65   (D) 35   (E) 55.

4. Dan spent 2/3 of his money at the first store and spent 1/7 of the money at the second store. What fraction of the total money did he spend?
(A) 2/23   (B) 11/21   (C) 17/21   (D) 3/10   (E) 1/2

5. In the diagram, all angles are right angles and the lengths of the sides are given in centimeters. Note the diagram is not drawn to scale. What is X, in centimeters?
(A) 1   (B) 2   (C) 5   (D) 4   (E) 3

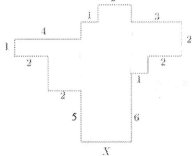

6. A rectangular photograph is placed in a frame that forms a border four inches wide on all sides of the photograph. The photograph measures 11 inches high and 17 inches wide. Find the area of the border, in square inches.
(A) 356   (B) 400   (C) 475   (D) 187   (E) 288

American Math Competition 8 Practice — Test 2

7. Cathy must take four 100-point tests in her math class. Her goal is to achieve an average grade of at least 93 on the tests. Her first two test scores were 94 and 90. After seeing her score on the third test, she realized that she could still reach her goal. What is the lowest possible score she could have made on the third test?
(A) 90 (B) 88 (C) 89 (D) 96 (E) 97

8. On Monday, Newton's Bakery discounted the price of pies 20%. On Tuesday, it discounted the pies an additional 20%. What is the combined percent discount?
(A) 40 (B) 64 (C) 30 (D) 36 (E) 10

9. The Zoo has a number of chickens and a number of rabbits. On one visit to the zoo, Mary counted 343 heads and 1024 legs. How many of the animals that Mary counted were rabbits?
(A) 61 (B) 122 (C) 169 (D) 150 (E) 161

10. How many 5-digit numbers greater than 10000 are there that use the five digits of 20123?
(A) 24 (B) 48 (C) 120 (D) 72 (E) 12

11. The mean, median, and unique mode of the positive integers $1, 5, 6, 7, 7, 9, x$ are all equal. What is the value of x?
(A) 7 (B) 6 (C) 11 (D) 14 (E) 12

12. Find the units digit of $3^{2013} - 2^{2015}$.
(A) 5 (B) 3 (C) 1 (D) 7 (E) 9

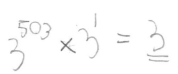

American Math Competition 8 Practice Test 2

13. James bought some pencils at the school bookstore and paid $2.47. Charles bought some of the same pencils and paid $3.23. How many more pencils did Charles buy than James?
(A) 2   (B) 3   (C) 4   (D) 5   (E) 6

14. In the BIG N, a middle school football conference, each team plays every other team exactly twice. If a total of 132 conference games were played during the 2012 season, how many teams were members of the BIG N conference?
(A) 11   (B) 12   (C) 8   (D) 9   (E) 10

15. The smallest positive integer that has 2 as a remainder when divided by 3, 4, 5, 6, 7, 8 lies between what numbers?
(A) 400 and 450   (B) 500 and 550   (C) 700 and 750   (D) 800 and 850   (E) 900 and 950

16. Each of the digits 4, 5, 6, 7, 8, and 9 is used only once to make two three-digit numbers so that they have the largest possible product. Which of the following could be the product?
(A) 645498   (B) 847240   (C) 843500   (D) 844200   (E) 809622

17. A square with an integer side length is cut into 19 squares, all of which have integer side length and at least 16 of which have area 1. What is the smallest possible value of the length of the side of the original square?
(A) 4   (B) 5   (C) 8   (D) 6   (E) 7

18. What is the smallest positive integer that is neither prime nor square and that has no prime factor less than 100?
(A) 10403   (B) 13133   (C) 10201   (D) 13139   (E) 31149

19. In a jar of red, green, and blue marbles, all but 16 are red marbles, all but 28 are green, and all but 34 are blue. How many marbles are in the jar?
(A) 26 (B) 28 (C) 39 (D) 40 (E) 5

20. What is the correct ordering of the three numbers $\frac{7}{13}$, $\frac{9}{17}$, and $\frac{15}{29}$, in increasing order?

(A) $\frac{15}{29} < \frac{7}{13} < \frac{9}{17}$ (B) $\frac{15}{29} < \frac{9}{17} < \frac{7}{13}$ (C) $\frac{7}{13} < \frac{9}{17} < \frac{15}{29}$ (D) $\frac{9}{17} < \frac{15}{29} < \frac{7}{13}$

(E) $\frac{9}{17} < \frac{7}{13} < \frac{15}{29}$

21. Mark has a large white cube that has an edge of 20 feet. He also has enough red paint to cover 1800 square feet. Mark uses all the paint to create a white circle centered on each face, surrounded by a red border. Find the area of one of the white circles, in square feet.
(A) $200\sqrt{2}$ (B) 200π (C) $100\sqrt{2}$ (D) 100 (E) 100π

22. Let R be a set of nine distinct integers. Six of the elements of the set are 5, 6, 7, 9, 12, and 17. What is the number of possible values of the median of R?

(A) 4 (B) 5 (C) 6 (D) 7 (E) 8

23. An equilateral triangle and a regular hexagon have equal areas. If the perimeter of the hexagon is 12, what is the perimeter of the equilateral triangle?
(A) 6 (B) 5 (C) $6\sqrt{6}$ (D) $6\sqrt{3}$ (E) $3\sqrt{6}$

24. A circle of radius 5 is cut into four congruent arcs. The four arcs are joined to form the star figure shown. Find the ratio of the area of the star figure to the area of the original circle.

(A) $\frac{4}{\pi} - 1$ (B) $\frac{\pi - 1}{\pi}$ (C) $\frac{1}{\pi}$ (D) $\frac{\sqrt{3}}{\pi}$ (E) $\frac{4}{\pi}$

25. A square with side of 7 is inscribed in a square with side length 9, with one vertex of the smaller square on each side of the larger square. A vertex of the smaller square divides a side of the larger square into two segments, one of length x and the other of length y. Find the value of xy.
(A) 15 (B) 25 (C) 16 (D) 12 (E) 14

American Math Competition 8 Practice   Test 2

SOLUTIONS:

1. Solution: (E):
Set up a proportion to compare the two ratios of number of minutes to number of jars.
$$\frac{8}{3} = \frac{24}{x} \Rightarrow \frac{1}{3} = \frac{3}{x}.$$
Solving for x, $x = 9$ minutes.

2. Solution: (B).
The net increase per day is 8 worms − 6 worms = 2 worms. There are typically 365 days in a year, so the number of worms grows by about $2 \times 365 = 730$, or close to 700 worms a year.

3. Solution: (B).
From 9:20 am to 12:00 noon is 2 hours and 40 minutes, or 160 minutes. Because 45 minutes already passed, 115 minutes remain.

4. Solution: (C) 17/21.
The total amount of money is was 1. The fraction of the money Dan spent was
$$\frac{2}{3} + \frac{1}{7} = \frac{17}{21}.$$

5. Solution: (E).
The horizontal sides on the bottom add up to $7 + X$ while the horizontal sides on the top add up to 10. Therefore $X = 3$.

6. Solution: (E).
The width of the frame is $17 + 4 + 4 = 25$ inches, and its height is $11 + 4 + 4 = 19$ inches. It encloses an area of $25 \times 19 = 475$ square inches. The photograph occupies $11 \times 17 = 187$ square inches of that area, so the area of the border itself is $475 - 187 = 288$ square inches

7. Solution: (B).
To achieve an average grade of 93 on the four tests, Cathy must score a total of $4 \times 93 = 372$ points. She scored a total of $94 + 90 = 184$ points on her first two tests, so she must score a total of at least $372 - 184 = 188$ points on her last two tests.

Because she can score at most 100 on her fourth test, she must have scored at least 88 on her third test.

8. Solution (D): The price of an item costing d after both discounts are applied is $0.80(0.80d) = 0.64d$, a discount of 36% off the original price.

9. Solution: (C).
All 343 heads belonged to animals with at least two legs, accounting for 686 of the 1024 legs. The additional 338 legs belonged to 169 rabbits, each of which had two additional legs. So Mary saw 169 rabbits.

10. Solution (B).
To form a number greater than 10000, the first digit must be 1, 2, or 3. If the first digit is a 1, we have 4!/2 = 24/2 = 12 ways to arrange the remaining four digits.

If the first digit is a 2, we have 4! = 24 ways to arrange the remaining four digits.

If the first digit is a 3, we have 4!/2 = 12 ways to arrange the remaining four digits.

So the answer is 12 + 24 + 12 = 48.

11. Solution: (D).
Because the mode is unique, it must be 7, so the mean must also be 7.
The sum of the seven numbers is $35 + x$, which must be equal to
$7 \times 7 = 49$. Therefore $x = 14$. The median of the numbers 1, 5, 6, 7, 7, 9, 14 is also 7.

12. Solution: (A).
Looking for pattern, the last digit of 3^n is repeating every four digits: 3, 9, 7, 1.

The last digit of 2^n is repeating every four digits as well: 2, 4, 8, 6.

So the last digit of $3^{2013} = 3^{503 \times 4 + 1}$ is the same as the last digit of 3^1. The last digit of 3^{2013} is 3.

The last digit of $2^{2015} = 2^{503 \times 4 + 3}$ is the same as the last digit of 2^3. So the last digit of 2^{2015} is 8. So the answer is 13 – 8 = 5.

American Math Competition 8 Practice Test 2

13. Solution: (C).
Method 1:
Since $2.47 = 247 ¢ = 19 \times 13$ and $3.23 = 323¢ = 19 \times 17$, the pencils cost 19 cents each. That means Charles James bought $17 - 13 = 4$ pencils more than James.

Method 2:
$323 - 247 = 76 = 4 \times 19$. The pencils cost 19 cents each and Charles bought 4 more pencils than James.

14. Solution: (B) 12.
Since there are two teams involved with each game, the total number of games n teams will play is $2\binom{n}{2} = 2 \times \frac{n(n-1)}{2} = (n-1)n$.
Then we have $(n-1)n = 132 = 11 \times 12$.
So $n = 12$.

15. Solution: (D).
$3 = 3$
$4 = 2^2$
$5 = 5$
$6 = 2 \times 3$
$7 = 7$
$8 = 2^3$.

The least common multiple of them is $2^3 \times 7 \times 5 \times 3 = 840$.

So $840 + 2 = 842$ is the smallest number greater than 2 to leave a remainder of 2 when divided by 3, 4, 5, 6, 7, and 8.

Therefore the number lies between 800 and 850.

16. Solution: (C): 843500.
Step 1: We put the largest digits 9 and 8 in the leftmost boxes first.
□□□ : 9
□□□: 8

23

American Math Competition 8 Practice — Test 2

Step 2: We select the digit 6 to be attached to 9 and the digit 7 to be attached to the digit 8 (the smaller digit goes with the larger number).

☐☐☐ : **96**

☐☐☐ : **87**

Step 3: We select the digit 4 to be attached to 96 and the digit 5 to be attached to the digit 86 (the smaller digit goes with the larger number).

☐☐☐ : **964**

☐☐☐ : **875**

The greatest product is 843500.

17. Solution: (B).
The area of the original square is a square number that is more than 16, so 25 is the least possible value for the area of the original square. Its side has length 5. One possible way of cutting the square is shown below:

18. Solution (A):
Since the integer is neither prime nor square, it is divisible either by two distinct primes or by the cube of a prime. The smallest prime numbers not less than 100 are 101 and 103. Since $101 \times 103 = 10403 < 101^3$, the smallest number satisfying this description is 10403.

19. Solution: (C).
Let g, b, and r be the number of green, blue, and red marbles respectively. Then

$g + b = 16$ (1)

$r + b = 28$ (2)

$g + r = 34$ (3)

(1) + (2) + (3): $2(g + b + r) = 78$ ⇒ $g + b + r = 39$.

20. Solution: (B).

$$\frac{7}{13} \underset{119}{\overset{117}{\times}} \frac{9}{17} \quad \Rightarrow \quad \frac{9}{17} < \frac{7}{13}$$

$$\frac{15}{29} \underset{255}{\overset{261}{\times}} \frac{9}{17} \quad \Rightarrow \quad \frac{15}{29} < \frac{9}{17}.$$

The order is $\frac{15}{29} < \frac{9}{17} < \frac{7}{13}$.

21. Solution (D):
The surface area of the cube is $6 \times 20^2 = 2400$ square feet. The green paint covers 1800 square feet, so the total area of the white circles is $2400 - 1800 = 600$ square feet. There are 6 white circles, so each has area $600/6 = 100$ square feet.

22. Solution (D):
When we write all nine distinct integers in increasing order, the median, which is the middle number, would be in the fifth place.

17 cannot be the median. Even if all of the remaining integers are greater than 17, the median is 12 (5, 6, 7, 9, **12**, 17, 18, 19, 20).
If all of the remaining integers are less than 5, then the median is 6. So 5 could not be the median.

All the integers from 6 to 12 are possible medians, and their count is 7.
6:   2, 3, 4, 5, **6**, 7, 9, 12, 17
7:   3, 4, 5, 6, **7**, 9, 12, 13, 17
8:   4, 5, 6, 7, **8**, 9, 12, 13, 17
9:   5, 6, 7, 8, **9**, 12, 13, 14, 17
10: 5, 6, 7, 9, **10**, 12, 13, 14, 17
11: 5, 6, 7, 9, **11**, 12, 13, 14, 17

23. Solution (C):
Method 1:

The hexagon can be divided into 6 congruent smaller equilateral triangles, each with side length of 2, as shown. The area of each smaller equilateral triangle is $A_s = \dfrac{\sqrt{3}a^2}{4} = \dfrac{\sqrt{3} \times 2^2}{4} = \sqrt{3}$.

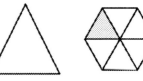

The area of the equilateral triangle is $6\sqrt{3}$ and the length of each side is b and $6\sqrt{3} = \dfrac{\sqrt{3}b^2}{4} \Rightarrow b = 2\sqrt{6}$.

The perimeter of the equilateral triangle is $3b = 3 \times 2\sqrt{6} = 6\sqrt{6}$.

Method 2:
Let the area of the hexagon be A. The hexagon can be divided into 6 congruent smaller equilateral triangles, each with side length of 2.
The equilateral triangle can be divided into 4 smaller congruent equilateral triangles, each with side length s.

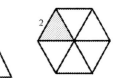

Then we have the ratio of their areas as follows:

$$\dfrac{\frac{A}{4}}{\frac{A}{6}} = (\dfrac{s}{2})^2 \quad \Rightarrow \quad \dfrac{6}{4} = \dfrac{s^2}{4} \quad \Rightarrow \quad s^2 = 6 \Rightarrow \quad s = \sqrt{6}$$

The perimeter of the equilateral triangle is $6s = 6\sqrt{6}$.

24. Solution: (A).
We draw a square and four circles congruent to the original circle and a square with four vertices as the centers of four circles, as shown.

The area of the original circle is $\pi(5^2) = 25\pi$.

The area of the square is $10^2 = 100$.

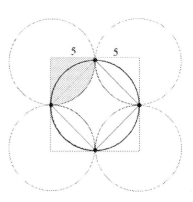

The area of the star figure = the area of the square $- 4 \times$ the area of the quarter circle
= the area of the square $-$ the area of the circle = $100 - 25\pi$.

American Math Competition 8 Practice — Test 2

The ratio of the area of the star figure to the area of the original circle is
$$\frac{100-25\pi}{25\pi} = \frac{4}{\pi} - 1.$$

25. Solution: (C).

Method 1:

The area of the region inside the larger square and outside the smaller square has total area $81 - 49 = 32$.

So $\frac{1}{2} xy \times 4 = 32 \quad \Rightarrow \quad xy = 16$.

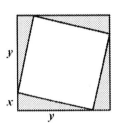

Method 2:

$x^2 + y^2 = 7^2$ \hfill (1)

$x + y = 9$ \hfill (2)

Squaring both sides of (2): $x^2 + 2xy + y^2 = 81$ \hfill (3)

(3) − (1): $2xy = 32 \quad \Rightarrow \quad xy = 16$.

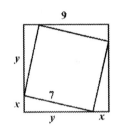

American Mathematics Competitions

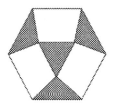

Practice 3

AMC 8

(American Mathematics Contest 8)

INSTRUCTIONS

1. DO NOT OPEN THIS BOOKLET UNTIL YOUR PROCTOR TELLS YOU.

2. This is a twenty-five question multiple choice test. Each question is followed by answers marked A, B, C, D and E. Only one of these is correct.

3. Mark your answer to each problem on the AMC 8 Answer Form with a #2 pencil. Check the blackened circles for accuracy and erase errors and stray marks completely. Only answers properly marked on the answer form will be graded.

4. There is no penalty for guessing. Your score on this test is the number of correct answers.

5. No aids are permitted other than scratch paper, graph paper, rulers, and erasers. No problems on the test will require the use of a calculator.

6. Figures are not necessarily drawn to scale.

7. Before beginning the test, your proctor will ask you to record certain information on the answer form.

8. When your proctor gives the signal, begin working on the problems. You will have 40 minutes to complete the test.

9. When you finish the exam, *sign your name* in the space provided on the Answer.

American Math Competition 8 Practice Test 3

1. At Hope Middle School the mathematics teachers are Miss Germain, Mr. Newton, and Mrs. Young. There are 18 students in Miss Germain's class. There are 8 more students in Mr. Newton's class than that in Miss Germain's class. The number of students in Mrs. Young's class is twice as many as the number of students in in Miss Germain's class. If all but one student are taking the AMC 8 Contest this year, how many students at Hope Middle School are taking the contest?

(A) 5476 (B) 72 (C) 79 (D) 34 (E) 76

2. If $a * b = \dfrac{a+b}{ab}$ for positive integers a and b, then what is $5 * 10$?

(A) $\dfrac{10}{3}$ (B) 10 (C) 3 (D) $\dfrac{3}{10}$ (E) 50

3. The graph shows the price of five gallons of gasoline during the first ten months of the year. By what percent is the highest price more than the lowest price?

(A) 100 (B) 88 (C) 70 (D) 66 (E) 50.

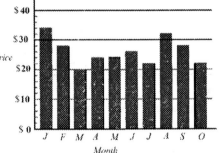

4. What is the sum of the mean, median, and mode of the numbers 3, 4, 1, 4, 2, 5, 1, 4?
(A) 9.5 (B) 10 (C) 10.5 (D) 11.5 (E) 12

5. Anna needs to replace a light bulb located 0.15 meters below the ceiling in her kitchen. The ceiling is 2.7 meters above the floor. Alice can reach 40 centimeters above the top of her head. Standing on a stool of 50 centimeters high, she can just reach the light bulb. What is Anna's height, in centimeters?
(A) 160 (B) 165 (C) 150 (D) 170 (E) 140

6. Which of the following figures has the greatest number of lines of symmetry?
(A) equilateral triangle
(B) square

29

American Math Competition 8 Practice   Test 3

(C) regular pentagon
(D) regular hexagon
(E) circle

7. Using only pennies, nickels, and quarters, what is the smallest number of coins Freddie would need so he could pay any amount of money up to 99 cents?
(A) 9   (B) 11   (C) 10   (D) 12   (E) 99

8. A car leaves a town traveling at 40 mph. Two hours later, a second car leaves the same town, on the same road, traveling 60 mph. The second car drives how many hours to overtake the first car?
(A) 2 hours   (B) 1 hour   (C) 1.5 hours   (D) 4 hours   (E) 3 hours

9. Sam got 95% of the problems correct on a 20-problem test, 96% on a 75-problem test, and 92% on a 25-problem test. What percent of all the problems did Sam answer correctly?
(A) 93   (B) 75   (C) 94   (D) 95   (E) 86

10. Five pepperoni circles will exactly fit across the diameter of a 10-inch pizza when placed as shown. If a total of 10 circles of pepperoni are placed on this pizza without overlap, what fraction of the pizza is covered by pepperoni?
(A) 1/2   (B) 4/5   (C) 2/3   (D) 1/3   (E) 2/5

11. The top of one tree is 22 feet higher than the top of another tree. The heights of the two trees are in the ratio 5 : 7. In feet, how tall is the taller tree?
A) 64   B) 77   (C) 80   (D) 96   (E) 112

12. Of the 640 balls in a large bag, 85% are red and the rest are blue. How many of the red balls must be removed from the bag so that 75% of the remaining balls are red?
(A) 250   (B) 500   (C) 275   (D) 256   (E) 150

American Math Competition 8 Practice   Test 3

13. The lengths of the sides of a triangle measured in inches are three consecutive even integers. The length of the shortest side is 25% of the perimeter. What is the length of the longest side?
(A) 4   (B) 6   (C) 9   (D) 12   (E) 10

14. What is the sum of the prime factors of 2013?
(A) 674   (B) 77   (C) 75   (D) 67   (E) 201

15. A jar contains five different colors of gum drops: 25% are blue, 30% are brown, 3% are red, 17% are yellow and the other 40 gum drops are green. If half of brown gum drops are replaced by blue gum drops, how many of the gum drops will be blue?
(A) 35   (B) 36   (C) 64   (D) 48   (E) 68

16. The area of a square is $\dfrac{16}{\pi}$ of the area of a circle. Find the ratio of the side length of the square to the diameter of the circle.
(A) 3   (B) 2   (C) π (D) $\sqrt{2\pi}$ (E) 4

17. The diagram shows an octagon consisting of 10 unit squares. The portion below PQ is a unit square and a triangle with base 5. Find the ratio QX/XP if PQ bisects the area of the octagon.
(A) $\dfrac{3}{4}$ (B) $\dfrac{1}{2}$ (C) $\dfrac{2}{3}$ (D) $\dfrac{3}{5}$ (E) $\dfrac{2}{5}$

18. A decorative shape is made up of a rectangle with semicircles on each end. The ratio of AD to AB is 7 : 4 and AB = 40 inches. Find the ratio of the area of the rectangle to the combined areas of the semicircles.
(A) 7 : 4   (B) 3 : 2   (C) $\dfrac{112}{65\pi}$ (D) $\dfrac{30}{\pi}$ (E) $\dfrac{37}{19\pi}$

19. The two circles are concentric circles with center *C*. Chord *AB* is tangent to the inner circle at *D* and *AB* = 22. Find the area between the two circles.
(A) 144π. (B) 100π. (C) 121π. (D) 169π.

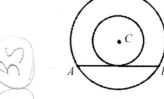

20. In a room, 6/7 of all the people are wearing gloves, and 5/9 of the people are wearing hats. What is the minimum number of people in the room wearing both a hat and gloves?
(A) 54 (B) 36 (C) 26 (D) 36 (E) 68

21. Ping is an avid reader. She bought a copy of the bestseller Math is Fun. On the first day, Ping read 2/5 of the pages plus 53 more, and on the second day she read 3/7 of the remaining pages, plus 12 pages. On the third day, she read 1/4 of the remaining pages, plus 8 pages. She then realized that there were only 16 pages left to read, which she read the next day. How many pages are in this book?
(A) 120 (B) 180 (C) 220 (D) 300 (E) 360

22. The hundreds digit of a three-digit number is 7 more than the units digit. The digits of the three-digit number are reversed, and the resulting number is subtracted from the original three-digit number. What is the units digit of the final result?
(A) 0 (B) 2 (C) 4 (D) 6 (E) 3

23. As shown in the figure, semicircles *POQ* and *ROS* pass through the center of circle *O*. What is the shaded area?
(A) 24 (B) 8 (C) $12 - 2\pi$ (D) $24 - 2\pi$
(E) $12 - 4\pi$

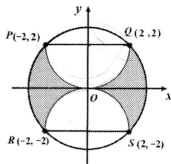

American Math Competition 8 Practice Test 3

24. What is the correct ordering of the three numbers 2^{40}, 3^{28}, and 4^{19}?
(A) $4^{19} < 2^{40} < 3^{28}$.   (B) $4^{19} < 3^{28} < 2^{40}$.   (D) $3^{28} < 4^{19} < 2^{40}$.
(B) $3^{28} < 2^{40} < 4^{19}$.   (E) $2^{40} < 4^{19} < 3^{28}$.

25. Every day at school, Alex climbs a total of 8 stairs. Alex can take stairs 1, 2, 3, or 4 at a time. For example, Alex could climb 3, then 1, then 4 stairs. In how many ways can Alex climb the 8 stairs?
(A) 56   (B) 18   (C) 20   (D) 22   (E) 108

American Math Competition 8 Practice Test 3

SOLUTIONS:

1. Solution: (C).
The total number of students taking the test is $18 + (18 + 8) + 2(18) = 80$.
$80 - 1 = 79$.

2. Solution: (D).
$a * b = \dfrac{a+b}{ab} = \dfrac{5+10}{5 \times 10} = \dfrac{15}{50} = \dfrac{3}{10}$.

3. Solution (C): The highest price in January was $34 and the lowest in March was $20.
$\dfrac{34 - 20}{20} = 0.7 = 70\%$

4. Solution (C): Arrange the numbers in increasing order: 1, 1, 2, 3, 4, 4, 4, 5. The mean is the sum divided by 8, or 24/8 = 3. The median is halfway between 3 and 4, or 3.5. The mode is 4, because there are more 4's than any other number. The sum of the mean, median, and mode is $3 + 3.5 + 4 = 10.5$.

5. Solution: (B).
Let Anna's height be x centimeters.
$50 + x + 40 + 15 = 270 \quad \Rightarrow \quad x = 165$ cm.

6. Solution: (E).
The number of lines of symmetry for the figures:
an equilateral triangle: 3; a square: 4; a regular pentagon: 5; a regular hexagon: 6; and a circle: infinite many lines of symmetry.

7. Solution: (B).
Let p, n, and q be the number of pennies, nickels, and quarters, respectively.
$p + 5n + 25q \leq 99$
So we need at least 4 pennies to make small change (1, 2, 3, and 4 cents). Adding two nickels means that change up to fourteen cents can be made. Adding two more nickels

extends the changes to 24. Adding a quarter extends the change to 49 cents. Adding two more quarters permits any amount of change up to $0.99.
4 pennies+ 4 nickels + 3 quarters = 11 coins worth $0.99

8. Solution: (D).
Denote the first car's speed as r_B and second car's speed as r_A with $r_A > r_B$. Let the distance between them be d.
One may think that the first car is not moving, and that second car travels at a relative speed of $(r_A - r_B)$ to cover the distance d in time t.
Within two hours, the first car travles a distance of 2×40 miles.
By the distance formula $d = (r_A - r_B)t$, $80 = (60 - 40)t$ $\Rightarrow$ $t = 4$ hours.

9. Solution: (D).
The three tests contain a total of 120 problems. Sam received 95% of 20 = 19, 96% of 75 = 72, and 92% of 25 = 23. Sam correctly answered 19 + 72 + 23 = 114 problems.

The percent of problems Sam answered correctly was: $\dfrac{114}{120} = 0.95 = 95\%$

10. Solution: (E).
If 5 pepperonis fit across the diameter, then each pepperoni is $\pi(1)^2 = \pi$ square inches. The 10 pepperoni circles cover 10π square inches of the pizza. The area of the pizza is $\pi(5)^2 = 25\pi$ square inches. The fraction of the pizza covered by pepperoni is $\dfrac{10\pi}{25\pi} = \dfrac{2}{5}$.

11. Solution: (B):
Let x be the height of the taller tree and y be the height of the other tree.
$\dfrac{y}{x} = \dfrac{5}{7}$ $\Rightarrow$ $y = \dfrac{5}{7}x$ (1)
$x - y = 22$ (2)
Substituting (1) into (2): $x - \dfrac{5}{7}x = 22$ $\Rightarrow$ $\dfrac{2}{7}x = 22$ $\Rightarrow$ $x = 7 \times 11 = 77$

12. Solution: (D):

American Math Competition 8 Practice   Test 3

The number of red balls in the bag is $640 \times 85\% = 544$. After x red balls are removed, we have $\dfrac{544-x}{640-x} = \dfrac{75}{100} = \dfrac{75 \times 6.4}{100 \times 6.4} = \dfrac{544-x-480}{640-x-640} = \dfrac{x-64}{x} = \dfrac{3}{4} \Rightarrow x = 256.$
So 256 red balls must be removed.

13. Solution: (E):
Let three sides be $2x - 2, 2x, 2x + 2$.

$2x - 2 = 0.25 (2x - 2 + 2x + 2x + 2) \Rightarrow 2x - 2 = 0.25 (6x) \Rightarrow 2x - 2 = 1.5x$
$\Rightarrow 0.5x = 2 \Rightarrow x = 4.$
Thus $2x + 2 = 2 \times 4 + 2 = 10$.

14. Solution: (C).
The sum of the digits is $2 + 1 + 0 + 3 = 6$. So 2013 is divisible by 3.
$2013 = 3 \times 671$.
Since $6 + 1 = 7$, 671 is divisible by 11.
$2013 = 3 \times 671 = 3 \times 11 \times 61$.
The sum of the prime factors is $3 + 11 + 61 = 75$.

15. Solution: (C):
The 40 green gum drops are $100\% - (25 + 30 + 3 + 17)\% = 25\%$ of the total gum drops, so there are 160 gum drops in the jar. The number of blue gum drops is 25% of 160, which is 40, and the number of brown gum drops is 30% of 160, which is 48. After half the brown gum drops are replaced by blue ones, the number of blue gum drops is $24 + 40 = 64$.

16. Solution: (B).
Let the side length of the square be a and the diameter of the corcle be d.
$a^2 = \dfrac{16}{\pi} \times \dfrac{1}{4}\pi d^2 \Rightarrow a^2 = 4d^2 \Rightarrow \dfrac{a^2}{d^2} = 4 \Rightarrow \dfrac{a}{d} = 2.$

17. Solution: (D). $\dfrac{3}{5}$.
The area below PQ is

$1 + \frac{1}{2} \times 5 \times (QY + 1) = 5 \quad \Rightarrow \quad QY = \frac{3}{5}.$

ΔXYQ is similar to ΔXSP.

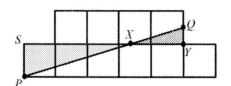

$\frac{QY}{PS} = \frac{QX}{XP} \quad \Rightarrow \quad \frac{\frac{3}{5}}{1} = \frac{QX}{XP} \quad \Rightarrow \quad \frac{QX}{XP} = \frac{3}{5}.$

18. Solution: (C).

The given ratio implies that $AD = 70$ inches, so the area of the rectangle is $AB \times AD = 40 \times 70 = 2800$ square inches. The 4 semicircles make 2 circle with radius = 20 and radius = 35 inches, respectively. The areas of the circle are $400\pi + 1225\pi = 1625\pi$.

The ratio of the areas is $\frac{2800}{1625\pi} = \frac{112}{65\pi}$.

19. Solution: (C).

Connect AC. Draw $CD \perp AB$ at B. CD is the perpendicular bisector of AB. So $AD = 22/2 = 11$.

Triangle ACD is a right triangle.
By the Pythagorean Theorem, $AC^2 - CD^2 = AD^2$ (1)
$\pi \times$ (1): $\pi \times AC^2 - \pi \times CD^2 = \pi \times AD^2$ (2)

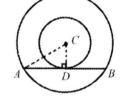

Note that left hand side of (2) is exactly the area between the circles.
So the answer is $\pi \times AD^2 = \pi \times 11^2 = 121\pi$.

20. Solution: (C).

Because 6/7 and 5/9 of the people in the room are whole numbers, the number of people in the room is a multiple of both 7 and 9. The least common multiple of 7 and 9 is 63, so the minimum number of people in the room is 63.

6/7 of all the people are wearing gloves: $\frac{6}{7} \times 63 = 54$ people are wearing gloves.

5/9 of the people are wearing hats: $\frac{5}{9} \times 63 = 35$. Let x be the number of people in the room wearing both a hat and gloves. $63 = 54 + 35 - x \quad \Rightarrow \quad x = 26$.

21. Solution: (C).

We use the back –calculation method.

Let x be the number of pages in this book.

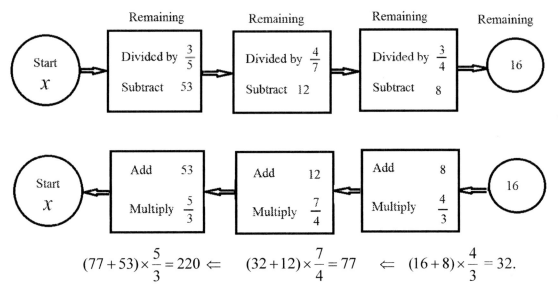

$$(77+53) \times \frac{5}{3} = 220 \Leftarrow (32+12) \times \frac{7}{4} = 77 \Leftarrow (16+8) \times \frac{4}{3} = 32.$$

The answer is 220 pages.

22. Solution: (E)
The original number can be written as $100a + 10b + c$.
The new number is $100c + 10b + a$.
The difference is $100a + 10b + c - (100c + 10b + a) = 100(a - c) + c - a$
We are given that $a - c = 7$.
So $100(a - c) + c - a = 100(a - c) - (a - c) = 700 - (7) = 693$.
So the units digit is 3.

23. Solution: (B).
Connect PR, PQ, QS, and RS. $PQSR$ is a square as shown in figure 2. The radius of semicircles POQ is $r = 2$ and the radius of semicircles ROS is $R = 2\sqrt{2}$.
The shaded area in figure 2 = $(S_{PQSR} - \pi r^2) \div 2 = 8 - 2\pi$.

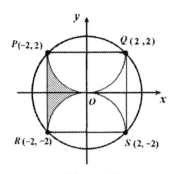
Figure 2

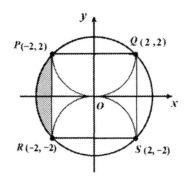
Figure 3

The shaded area in figure 3 = $\dfrac{\pi R^2 - S_{PQSR}}{4} = \dfrac{\pi(2\sqrt{2})^2 - 16}{4} = 2\pi - 4$.

The answer is $(8 - 2\pi + 2\pi - 4) \times 2 = 8$.

24. Solution: (A).
By the power rule $(a^m)^n = a^{mn}$, $2^{40} = (2^{10})^4$ and $3^{28} = (3^7)^4$.
$2^{10} = 1024$ and $3^7 = 2187$
Since $2187 > 1024$, 2^{40} is smaller than 3^{28}.
$4^{19} = (2^2)^{19} = 2^{38} < 2^{40}$.
So the correct ordering of the three numbers 2^{40}, 3^{28}, and 4^{19} is $4^{19} < 2^{40} < 3^{28}$.

25. Solution: (E) 108.
This is the case We need to get N_1, N_2, N_3, and N_4 in order to get N_5.
$N_5 = N_4 + N_3 + N_2 + N_1$

Stairs   # of ways   Note
4   8   1 + 1 + 1 + 1, 1 + 1 + 2, 1 + 3, 2 + 2, 4 (eight ways when ordering).
3   4   1 + 1 + 1, 1 + 2, 2 + 1, 3 (four ways)
2   2   1 + 1, or 2 (two ways)
1   1   1 (one way)

With the formula $N_5 = N_4 + N_3 + N_2 + N_1$, the sequence can be obtained as follows: 1, 2, 4, 8, 15, 29, 56, 108.

American Math Competition 8 Practice   Test 4

American Mathematics Competitions

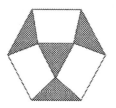

Practice 4
AMC 8

(American Mathematics Contest 8)

INSTRUCTIONS

1. DO NOT OPEN THIS BOOKLET UNTIL YOUR PROCTOR TELLS YOU.

2. This is a twenty-five question multiple choice test. Each question is followed by answers marked A, B, C, D and E. Only one of these is correct.

3. Mark your answer to each problem on the AMC 8 Answer Form with a #2 pencil. Check the blackened circles for accuracy and erase errors and stray marks completely. Only answers properly marked on the answer form will be graded.

4. There is no penalty for guessing. Your score on this test is the number of correct answers.

5. No aids are permitted other than scratch paper, graph paper, rulers, and erasers. No problems on the test will require the use of a calculator.

6. Figures are not necessarily drawn to scale.

7. Before beginning the test, your proctor will ask you to record certain information on the answer form.

8. When your proctor gives the signal, begin working on the problems. You will have 40 minutes to complete the test.

9. When you finish the exam, *sign your name* in the space provided on the Answer.

American Math Competition 8 Practice Test 4

1. Marty made three purchases for $1.92, $5.07 and $9.86. What was the change she got if she had a $20 bill to the nearest dollar?
(A) $10 (B) $ 5 (C) $ 4 (D) $3 (E) $8

2. On a math contest a student's score is the number of problems answered correctly minus the number of question unanswered. Bob answers 23 questions correctly, answers 4 questions incorrectly and doesn't answer the last 3. What is his score?
(A) 23 (B) 3 (C) 20 (D) 19 (E) 26

3. Lisa swims laps in the swimming pool. When she first started, she completed 12 laps in 30 minutes. Now she can finish 30 laps in 45 minutes. By how many minutes has she improved her lap time?
(A) 1 (B) 2 (C) 1/2 (D) 2/3 (E) 3

4. Initially, a spinner points north. Charles moves it clockwise $56\frac{3}{4}$ revolutions and then counterclockwise $26\frac{1}{8}$ revolutions. In what direction does the spinner point after the two moves?
(A) north (B) southwest (C) northwest (D) west (E) northeast

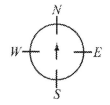

5. Points A, B, C and D are midpoints of the sides of the larger square. The smallest square is formed the same way. If the largest square has area 160, what is the area of the smallest square?
(A) 30 (B) 35 (C) 24 (D) 40 (E) 60

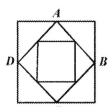

American Math Competition 8 Practice — Test 4

6. The letter T is formed by placing four 3 inch × 10 inch rectangles as shown. What is the perimeter of the T, in inches?
   (A) 32 (B) 44 (C) 52 (D) 50 (E) 54

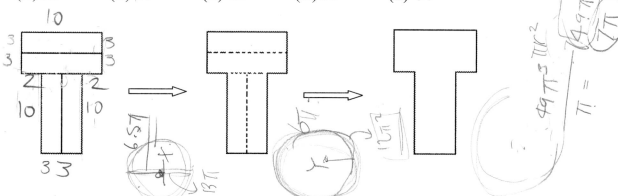

7. Circle X has a diameter of 13π. Circle Y has a circumference of $12\pi^2$. Circle Z has an area of $49\pi^3$. List the circles in order from smallest to largest radius.
   (A) X, Y, Z (B) Y, X, Z (C) Y, Z, X (D) Z, Y, X (E) X, Z, Y

8. The table shows some of the results of a survey by TV station KMCA. What percentage of the females surveyed watched the station?

	Watch	Don't Watch	Total
Male	95	?	120
Female	?	45	?
Total	200	70	270

   (A) 75 (B) 48 (C) 52 (D) 45 (E) 70

9. Find the product of $\dfrac{2}{1} \times \dfrac{3}{2} \times \dfrac{4}{3} \times \dfrac{5}{4} \times \cdots \times \dfrac{2014}{2013}$.
   (A) 1 (B) 1002 (C) 2014 (D) 2013 (E) 1001

10. George's teacher asks him to plot all the ordered pairs (w, l) of positive integers for which w is the width and l is the length of a rectangle with area 36. What should his graph look like?
    (A) A (B) B (C) C (D) D (E) E

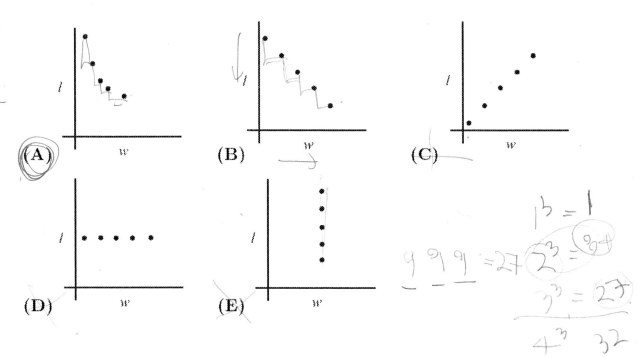

11. How many three-digit numbers have digits whose sum is a perfect cube?
(A) 13   (B) 26   (C) 36   (D) 38   (E) 39

12. Alex gets 90% on a 20-problem test, 95% on a 40-problem test and 96% on a 25-problem test. If the three tests are combined into one 85-problem test, which percent is closest to her overall score?
(A) 20   (B) 92   (C) 93   (D) 94   (E) 95

13. Cathy leaves Bluesboro at 6:30 AM heading for Greensboro on her bike. She bikes at a uniform rate of 8 miles per hour. Bob leaves Greensboro at 7:00 AM heading for Bluesboro on his bike. He bikes at a uniform rate of 12 miles per hour. They both bike on the same 34-mile route between Bluesboro and Greensboro. At what time in the morning do they meet?
(A) 7:50   (B) 8:00   (C) 7:30   (D) 8:30   (E) 9:30

American Math Competition 8 Practice — Test 4

14. Bob and Chan are reading the same 660-page novel. Bob reads a page in 30 seconds and Chan reads a page in 20 seconds. If Bob and Chan both read the whole book, Bob will spend how many more seconds reading than Chan?
(A) 7,600 (B) 6,600 (C) 12,500 (D) 15,200 (E) 22,800

15. Bob and Chan are reading the same 660-page novel, each with a copy of the book. Bob reads a page in 30 seconds and Chan reads a page in 20 seconds. They decide that they can save time by "team reading" the novel. In this scheme, Chan will read from page 1 to a certain page and Bob will read from the next page through page 660, finishing the book. What is the last page that Chan should read so that she and Bob spend the same amount of time reading the novel?
(A) 425 (B) 444 (C) 396 (D) 484 (E) 506

16. Three friends, Alice, Bob and Chan are reading the same 660-page novel. Alice reads a page in 10 seconds, Bob reads a page in 30 seconds and Chan reads a page in 20 seconds. If they divide the book into three sections so that each reads for the same length of time, how many seconds will each have to read?
(A) 2600 (B) 1600 (C) 6800 (D) 7000 (E) 3600

17. Joe rotates spinners P, Q and R and adds the resulting numbers. What is the probability that his sum is an even number?
(A) 3/4 (B) 2/3 (C) 1/2 (D) 1/3 (E) 1/4

18. A cube with 4-inch edges is made using 64 cubes with 1-inch edges. Fifty-six of the smaller cubes are grey and eight are white. If the eight white cubes are placed at the corners of the larger cube, what fraction of the surface area of the larger cube is grey?
(A) 1/12 (B) 1/9 (C) 1/6 (D) 1/4 (E) 1/8

19. Point D is the midpoint of both BC and AE of triangles ACB and ACE, respectively. The area of ACB is 11 square units. Find the area of triangle CDE in square units.
(A) 4   (B) 4.5   (C) 5   (D) 5.5   (E) 6

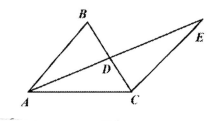

20. A singles tournament had six players: Alice, Betsy, Cathy, Debra, Emily, and Friday. Each player played every other player exactly twice, with no ties. If Alice won 8 games, Betsy won 6 games, Cathy won 4 games, Debra won 4 games and Emily won 4 games, how many games did Friday win?
(A) 0   (B) 1   (C) 4   (D) 3   (E) 2

21. An aquarium has a rectangular base that measures 120 cm by 60 cm and has a height of 70 cm. The aquarium is filled with water to a depth of 48 cm. A rock with volume 2016 cm^3 is then placed in the aquarium and completely submerged. By how many centimeters does the water level rise?
(A) 0.28   (B) 0.5   (C) 0.25   (D) 1.25   (E) 1

22. Four different one-digit positive integers are placed in the bottom row of cells. Numbers in adjacent cells are added and the sum is placed in the cell above them. In the second row, continue the same process to obtain a number in the top cell. What is the difference between the largest and smallest numbers possible in the top cell?
(A) 36   (B) 24   (C) 25   (D) 48   (E) 55

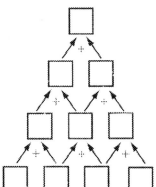

23. A box contains more than 1 and less than 1000 gold coins. If the coins are equally divided among six people, two coins are left over. If the coins are equally divided among seven people, three coins are left over. Find the sum of all possible number of coins in the box.

(A) 11,500 (B) 12,500 (C) 2,000 (D) 3,000 (E) 15,000

24. In the multiplication Below, A, B, C, D and E are different digits. What is A + B?

(A) 1 (B) 3 (C) 2 (D) 4 (E) 7

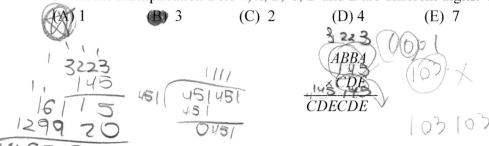

25. Barry wrote 6 different numbers less than 100, one on each side of 3 cards, and laid the cards on a table, as shown. The sums of the two numbers on each of the three cards are equal. The three numbers on the hidden sides are prime numbers. What is the greatest possible average of the two larger hidden prime numbers?

(A) 63 (B) 75 (C) 55 (D) 16 (E) 47

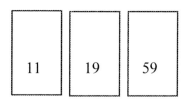

American Math Competition 8 Practice Test 4

SOLUTIONS:

1. Solution: (D).
Marty's total was approximately 2 + 5 + 10 = $17. She got 20 – 17 = $3.

2. Solution: (C).
Bob got 23 points for the questions he answered correctly. 23 – 3 = 20.

3. Solution: (A).
When Lisa started, she completed a lap in 30/12 = 2.5 minutes. Now she can complete a lap in 45/30 = 1.5 minutes. She has improved her lap time by 2.5 – 1.5 = 1 minute.

4. Solution: (B).
Method 1:
$56\frac{3}{4} - 26\frac{1}{8} = 30\frac{5}{8}$.

Ignore the number of complete revolutions because they do not affect direction.
The spinner points southwest.

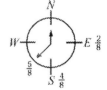

Method 2:
Ignore the number of complete revolutions because they do not affect direction.
Charles moves it clockwise $\frac{3}{4}$ revolutions and then counterclockwise $\frac{1}{8}$ revolutions. The spinner points southwest:

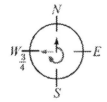

5. Solution: (D).
Divide the largest square into 16 congruent triangles, each triangle has area 16, as shown, 4 of which make up the smallest square.
So the smallest square has area 4 × 10 = 40.

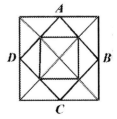

6. Solution: (C).
First, we view the figure from the left hand side and we see the
lengths (3 + 3 + 10) = 16. We can also view the figure from the right
hand side. So we get 16 × 2 = 32.

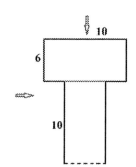

Second, we view the figure from the top and we see the lengths 10.
We can also view the figure from the bottom. So we get 10 × 2 = 20.

So the perimeter of the T is 32 + 20 = 52 inches.

7. Solution: (B).
We compare the diameters of the circles. Because circumference $C = \pi d$ and circle Y has circumference $12\pi^2$, its diameter is 12π. Because area $A = \frac{1}{4}\pi d^2$ and circle Z has area $49\pi^3$, its diameter is 14π. Ordering the diameters $12\pi < 13\pi < 14\pi$, so the circles in ascending order of radii length are Y, X and Z.

8. Solution: (E).
Because 270 − 120 = 150 of those surveyed were female, 150 − 45 = 105 of those surveyed are female watchers.

	Watch	Don't Watch	Total
Male	95	25	120
Female	105	45	150
Total	200	70	270

The percentage of females surveyed who watch KMCA is 105/150 × 100% = 70%.

9. Solution: (C).
Note that in each fraction, the numerator is the same as the denominator
$$\frac{2}{1} \times \frac{3}{2} \times \frac{4}{3} \times \frac{5}{4} \times \cdots \times \frac{2014}{2013} = 2014.$$

10. Solution: (A).
When the area of a rectangle is 36 square units and the sides are integers, the factors of 36 are the possible lengths of the sides. In point form, (w, l) could be (1, 36), (2, 18), (3, 12), (4, 9), and (6, 6). Only graph A fits these points.

American Math Competition 8 Practice Test 4

11. Solution: (D).
The sum of the digits of a three-digit number is at most $9 + 9 + 9 = 27$. This means the only possible perfect square sums are 1, 8, and 27. Each cube has the following three-digit possibilities:

1 :
100

8 :
800:   1
710:   4 (710, 701, 107, 170)
620:   4 (620, 602, 206, 260)
530:   4 (530, 503, 305, 350)
440:   2 (440, 404)

611:   3 (611, 116, 161)
521:   6 (521, 512, 251, 215, 125, 152).
431:   6
422:   3 (422, 242, 224)
332:   3 (332, 323, 233)

27:
999:   1.

There are $1 \times 3 + 2 + 3 \times 3 + 4 \times 3 + 6 \times 2 = 38$ three-digit numbers in all.

12. Solution: (D).
Note that 90% of 20 is 18, 95% of 40 is 38 and 96% of 25 is 24. Alex answers $18 + 38 + 24 = 80$ problems correctly out of 85 problems in all. His overall score is $80/85 \approx 94\%$.

13. Solution: (D).
Between 6:30 and 7:00 AM Cathy travels 4 miles. At 7:00 Cathy and Bob are only 30 miles apart. After 7:00, because they are both biking towards each other, the distance between them decreases at the rate of $8 + 12 = 20$ miles per hour. At that rate, it will take them $30/20 = 1.5$ hours to meet. So they will meet at 8:30 AM.

14. Solution: (B).
Bob takes $30 - 20 = 10$ more seconds per page than Chan. So the difference in their total reading times is $660 \cdot 10 = 6,600$ seconds. Bob will spend 6,600 more seconds reading than Chan.

15. Solution: (C).
If Chan reads x pages, she will read for $20x$ seconds. Bob has to read $660 - x$ pages, and this takes him $30(660 - x)$ seconds. Because Chan and Bob read the same amount of time, $20x = 30(660 - x) \Rightarrow 2x = 3(660 - x)$.
Solving for x,
$5x = 1980 \Rightarrow x = 396$.
So Chan will read the first 396 pages.

16. Solution: (E).
Method 1: The least common multiple of 10, 30 and 20 is 60. Using the LCM, in 60 seconds Alice reads $60/10 = 6$ pages, Chandra reads $60/20 = 3$ pages and Bob reads $60/30 = 2$ pages. Together they read a total of 11 pages in 60 seconds. The total number of seconds each reads is $\frac{660}{11} \cdot 60 = 3600$.

Method 2: Let a, b, and c be the number of pages each person reads, respectively.

$10a = 30b = 20c \Rightarrow \dfrac{a}{\frac{1}{10}} = \dfrac{b}{\frac{1}{30}} = \dfrac{c}{\frac{1}{20}} = \dfrac{a+b+c}{\frac{1}{10}+\frac{1}{30}+\frac{1}{20}} = \dfrac{10 \times 660}{1+\frac{1}{3}+\frac{1}{2}} = 3600$.

17. Solution: (B).
Because the sum of a number from spinner Q and a number from spinner R is always odd, the sum of the numbers on the three spinners will be even exactly when the number from spinner P is odd. So the probability of getting an even sum is 2/3.

18. Solution: (D).
Four white and 12 grey squares are visible on each of the six faces of the cube.
So $4/16 = 1/4$ of the surface will be white.

19. Solution: (D).

Method 1:
Connect BE. Because point D bisects both BC and AE, ABEC is a parallelogram. So BE // AC. So triangles ABD and ECD are congruent. Since BD = DC, the area of triangle ABD is $\frac{1}{2}$ of the area of triangle ABC, or 5.5. Thus the area of triangle CDE is 5.5 square units.

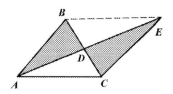

Method 2:
Because point D bisects both BC and AE, triangles ABD and ECD are congruent (BD = CD, AD = DE, ∠ADB = ∠EDC). Since BD = DC, the area of triangle ABD is $\frac{1}{2}$ of the area of triangle ABC, or 5.5. Thus the area of triangle CDE is 5.5 square units.

20. Solution: (C).
Each of the six players played 10 games, and each game involved two players. So there were $2 \times \binom{6}{2} = 30$ games (so there are 30 wins). Alice, Betsy, Cathy, Debra, and Emily won a total of 8 + 6 + 4 + 4 + 4 = 26 games, so Friday won 30 − 26 = 4 games.

21. Solution: (A).
Using the volume formula $lwh = V$, the volume of water in the aquarium is 120 × 60 × 48 = 345,600 cm³. When the rock is put in, the water and the rock will occupy a box-shaped region with volume 345,600 + 2016 = 347,616 cm³. The volume of the water and the rock is 120 × 60 × h, where h is the new height of the water. The new volume = 7200h = 347,616 cm³, so the new height is $h = \frac{347,616}{7200} = 48.28$

After adding the rock, the water rises 48.28 − 48 = 0.28 cm.

22. Solution: (D).
The number is the top cell is A + 3B + 3C + D.
The largest number is 7 + 3 × 8 + 3 × 9 + 6 = 64.
The smallest number is 3 + 3 × 1 + 3 × 2 + 4 = 16.

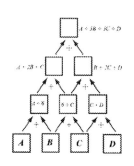

American Math Competition 8 Practice   Test 4

The difference is 64 − 16 = 48.

23. Solution: (A).
Integers that have a remainder of 2 when divided by 6 are 2, 8, 14, 20, 26, 32, 38, 42…

Integers that have a remainder of 3 when divided by 7 are 3, 10, 17, 24, 31, 38, 45…

The first integer that is common to both sequences is 38. The next integer will be 38 + LCM(6, 7) = 38 + 42 = 80.

The integers common to both sequences form an arithmetic sequence with a first term of 38 and a common difference of 42.
38 + 42(n − 1) ≤ 1000 ⇒ n ≤ 23. The sum of these 23 terms equals
23(76 + 22 × 42)/2 = 11500.

24. Solution: (A).
We can decompose $CDECDE = 1000CDE + CDE = 1001 \times CDE$. That means that $A = 1$ and $B = 0$. The sum is $1 + 0 = 1$.

25. Solution: (B).
Let the three hidden prime numbers be x, y, and z respectively.
$x + 11 = y + 19$ ⇒ $x − y = 8$.
The two prime numbers 71 and 79 (with a difference of 8) will have the greatest possible average. So $x = 79$ and $y = 71$. The average of 79 and 71 is 75.

The sum of two numbers in each card is 79 + 11 = 90. So 59 + z = 90 and z = 31.

Note: There are three sets: (79, 71, 31), (67, 59, 19), and (61, 53, 13). Only the first set yields the greatest possible average.

American Mathematics Competitions

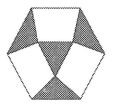

Practice 5
AMC 8
(American Mathematics Contest 8)

INSTRUCTIONS

1. DO NOT OPEN THIS BOOKLET UNTIL YOUR PROCTOR TELLS YOU.

2. This is a twenty-five question multiple choice test. Each question is followed by answers marked A, B, C, D and E. Only one of these is correct.

3. Mark your answer to each problem on the AMC 8 Answer Form with a #2 pencil. Check the blackened circles for accuracy and erase errors and stray marks completely. Only answers properly marked on the answer form will be graded.

4. There is no penalty for guessing. Your score on this test is the number of correct answers.

5. No aids are permitted other than scratch paper, graph paper, rulers, and erasers. No problems on the test will require the use of a calculator.

6. Figures are not necessarily drawn to scale.

7. Before beginning the test, your proctor will ask you to record certain information on the answer form.

8. When your proctor gives the signal, begin working on the problems. You will have 40 minutes to complete the test.

9. When you finish the exam, *sign your name* in the space provided on the Answer Form.

American Math Competition 8 Practice Test 5

1. On a map, a 24-centimeter length represents 144 kilometers. How many kilometers does a 34-centimeter length represent?
(A) 58   (B) 204   (C) 102   (D) 864   (E) 1224

2. How many different four-digit numbers can be formed by rearranging the four digits in 2014?
(A) 4   (B) 18   (C) 16   (D) 24   (E) 81

3. Twenty friends met for dinner at Oscar's Overstuffed Oyster House, and each ordered one meal. The portions were so large, there was enough food for 25 people. If they share, how many meals should they have ordered to have just enough food for the 20 of them?
(A) 16   (B) 9   (C) 10   (D) 15   (E) 18

4. Alex, Bob, Cathy, Danny, Emily, and Frank are chosen for the team to participate in the annual four-person-team basketball tournament. In how many ways can the four starters be chosen?
(A) 12   (B) 15   (C) 16   (D) 18   (E) 10

5. There are sixty teams compete in an annual basketball tournament. The losing team of each game is eliminated from the tournament. How many games will be played to determine the winner?
(A) 44   (B) 57   (C) 58   (D) 59   (E) 56

6. In an annual basketball tournament, Sally takes 30 shots and she has made 70% of her shots. After she takes 18 more shots, she raises her percentage to 75%. How many of the last 18 shots did she make?
(A) 11   (B) 12   (C) 15   (D) 14   (E) 18

7. Genia has 20% more money than Arizona, and Jamal has 20% less money than Arizona. What percent more money does Genia have than Jamal?
(A) 30   (B) 50   (C) 17   (D) 19   (E) 43

American Math Competition 8 Practice Test 5

8. Find the number of three-digit positive integers whose digits total 24.
(A) 9   (B) 10   (C) 8   (D) 7   (E) 6

9. The average of the 11 numbers in a list is 72. The average of the first two numbers is 18. What is the average of the last nine numbers?
(A) 65   (B) 56   (C) 83   (D) 84   (E) 60

10. Alex helped a neighbor 1.5 hours on Monday, 90 minutes on Tuesday, from 5:20 am to 9:10 on Wednesday morning, and 10 minutes on Friday. He is paid $11 per hour. How much did he earn for the week?
(A) $80   (B) $90   (C) $50   (D) $62   (E) $77

11. The numbers −8, 10, 12, 15 and 18 are rearranged according to these rules:
1. The median isn't first or last.
2. The largest isn't first, but it is in one of the first three places.
3. The smallest isn't last, but it is in one of the last three places.

What is the average of the first and last numbers?
(A) 9.5   (B) 9   (C) 12.5   (D) 13.5   (E) 14

12. Nancy usually leaves her cell phone on. If her cell phone is on but she is not actually using it, the battery will last for 120 hours. If she is using it constantly, the battery will last for only 15 hours. Since the last recharge, her phone has been on 45 hours, and during that time she has used it for 240 minutes. If she doesn't talk any more but leaves the phone on, how many more hours will the battery last?
(A) 57   (B) 47   (C) 120   (D) 37   (E) 43

13. Alex, Bob and Cathy are friends with different ages. Exactly one of the following statements is true.

I. Bob is the oldest.

II. Alex is not the oldest.
III. Cathy is not the youngest.

Rank the friends from the youngest to the oldest.
(A) Bob, Alex, Cathy (B) Alex, Bob, Cathy (C) Alex, Cathy, Bob,
(D) Cathy, Bob, Alex (E) Bob, Cathy, Alex

14. Find the area enclosed by the geoboard quadrilateral below? Note that the figure contains a "hole".
(A) 15 (B) 22.5 (C) 21.5 (D) 27
(E) 42

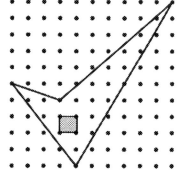

15. Thirteen black and twenty-four white hexagonal tiles were used to create the figure below. If a new figure is created by attaching a border of black tiles with the same size and shape as the others, how many black tiles are needed?
(A) 25 (B) 17 (C) 24 (D) 22 (E) 28

16. Two 1120 ml pitchers contain orange juice. One pitcher is 2/7 full and the other pitcher is 3/8 full. Water is added to fill each pitcher completely, then both pitchers are poured into one large container. What fraction of the mixture in the large container is orange juice?

(A) $\dfrac{7}{12}$ (B) $\dfrac{3}{16}$ (C) $\dfrac{37}{112}$ (D) $\dfrac{5}{56}$ (E) $\dfrac{3}{7}$

American Math Competition 8 Practice Test 5

17. Five friends have a total of 12 identical pencils, and each one has at least two pencils. In how many ways can this happen?
(A) 10   (B) 13   (C) 16   (D) 15   (E) 12

18. Five friends compete in a dart-throwing contest. Each one has two darts to throw at the same circular target, and each individual's score is the sum of the scores in the target regions that are hit. The scores for the target regions are the whole numbers 1 through 10. Each throw hits the target in a region with a different value. The scores are: Alice 12 points, Ben 4 points, Cindy 8 points, Dave 13 points, and Ellen 18 points. Who hits the region worth 7 points?
(A) Alice   (B) Ben   (C) Cindy   (D) Dave   (E) Ellen

19. A whole number larger than 2 leaves a remainder of 3 when divided by each of the numbers 4, 5, 6 and 7. The smallest such number lies between which two numbers?
(A) 300 and 350   (B) 400 and 450   (C) 200 and 229
(D) 100 and 149   (E) 500 and 569

20. Four-Ninths of the people in a room are seated in Seven-Elevenths of the chairs. The rest of the people are standing. If there are 16 empty chairs, how many people are in the room?
(A) 42   (B) 38   (C) 24   (D) 63   (E) 66

21. Spinners A and B are spun. On each spinner, the arrow is equally likely to land on each number. What is the probability that the sum of the two spinners' numbers is odd?

(A) 1/4   (B) 1/3   (C) 1/5   (D) 1/2   (E) 3/4

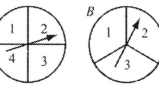

22. At a special party there are only single women, married men with their wives, and two babies for each couple. The probability that a randomly selected woman is single is 4/11. What fraction of the people in the room are babies?
(A) 4/11   (B) 7/16   (C) 3/8   (D) 5/12   (E) 7/30

23. Tim runs counterclockwise around square block *ADCB*. He lives at corner *A*. Which graph could represent his straight-line distance from home?

(A) 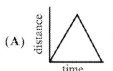 (B) (C) (D) 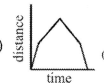 (E)

24. In the figure, the larger one of the two squares next to each other has the side length of 20 cm. Find the shaded area.
(A) 100 (B) 150 (C) 200 (D) 300 (E) undetermined.

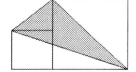

25. Two 20 × 20 squares intersect at right angles, bisecting their intersecting sides, as shown. The circle's diameter is the segment between the two points of intersection. What is the area of the shaded region created by removing the circle from the squares?
(A) $160 - 50\pi$ (B) $200 - 50\pi$ (C) $280 - 40\pi$
(D) $700 - 50\pi$ (E) $500 - 25\pi$

American Math Competition 8 Practice Test 5

SOLUTIONS:

1. Solution: (B).
If 24 centimeters represents 144 kilometers, then 1 centimeter represents 6 kilometers. So 34 centimeters represents $34 \times 6 = 204$ kilometers.

2. Solution: (B).
To form a four-digit number using 2, 0, 1 and 4, the digit in the thousands place can be 1, 2 or 4. There are three places available for the remaining digits. By the Fundamental Counting Principle, we get: $\underline{3} \times \underline{3} \times \underline{2} \times \underline{1} = 18$.
So 18 numbers are possible.

3. Solution: (A).
Let x be the number of meals they should have ordered. Then,

$20/25 = x/20 \quad \Rightarrow \quad x = 16.$

4. Solution: (B).
When four players start, two are the alternates. We have $\binom{6}{4} = \binom{6}{2} = \dfrac{6 \times 5}{2} = 15$ to select four starters.

5. Solution: (D).
It takes 59 games to eliminate 59 teams.

6. Solution: (C).
If Sally makes 70% of her 30 shots, she makes $0.70 \times 30 = 21$ shots. If Sally makes 75% of her $(30 + 18) = 48$ shots, she makes $0.75 \times 48 = 36$ shots. So she makes $36 - 21 = 15$ of the last 18 shots.

7. Solution: (B).
Let G, A, and J be the amount of money Genia, Arizona, and Jamal have, respectively.
$G = 1.2A$ \hfill (1)
$J = 0.8A$ \hfill (2)

American Math Competition 8 Practice   Test 5

$(1) \div (2)$: $G = 1.5J$.
Thus the amount of money Genia has is 50% more money than Jamal's money.

8. Solution: (B).
$24 = 9 + 9 + 6$: 3 numbers (996, 969, 699).
$24 = 9 + 8 + 7$: 6 numbers (987, 978, 897, 879, 798, 789)
$24 = 8 + 8 + 8$: 1 number.
There are 10 three-digit numbers whose digits sum to 24.

9. Solution: (D).
The sum of all five numbers is $11 \times 72 = 792$. The sum of the first two numbers is $2 \times 18 = 36$, so the sum of the last nine numbers is $792 - 36 = 756$. The average of the last three numbers is $756/9 = 84$.

10. Solution: (E).
Alex worked 1.5 hours on Monday, $1\frac{1}{2}$ hours on Tuesday, 3 hours and 50 minutes on Wednesday and 10 minutes on Friday, for a total of 7 hours. He earned $7 \times \$11 = \$77$.

11. Solution: (C).
The largest, smallest and median occupy the three middle places, so the other two numbers, 15 and 10, are in the first and last places. The average of 15 and 10 is 12.5.

12. Solution: (B).
By talking for 4 hours, the talking life of the battery left is $15 - 4 = 11$ hours.

Let x be the battery's life remaining if the phone is on and unused. Fifteen talking hours are equivalent to 120 on and unused hours. So by the proportion:

$\frac{15}{120} = \frac{11}{x}$ $\Rightarrow$ $x = 88$ hours.

Since the last recharge, her phone has been on 45 hours. Note that during the 45 hours, the phone is used $240/60 = 4$ hours and left on and unused for $45 - 4 = 41$ hours. So the battery will last $88 - 41 = 47$ hours if she doesn't talk any more but leaves the phone on.

American Math Competition 8 Practice   **Test 5**

13. Solution: (E).
We have two methods to solve this kind of problems:
(1) Find two statements that are contradicted to each other
(2) Find two statements that are in agreement with each other

We use (2) to solve this problem.
We see that I and II are in agreement. If Bob is the oldest, then Alex is not the oldest. But we know that there is only one statement is true. So this true statement must be III. Cathy is not the youngest and she can be either the oldest or the middle one. Since both I and II are false, we know that Alex is the oldest and Bob is not. So the order from the youngest to the oldest is: Bob, Cathy, Amy.

14. Solution: (C).
Method 1:
We just ignore the hole.

By Pick's Theorem, A, the area of a polygon is $A = \frac{B}{2} + I - 1$.

B is the number of lattice points on the boundary and I is the number of lattice points inside the polygon, not touching any of the sides. n is the number of holes inside the polygon.

In this case, the area is $A = \frac{B}{2} + I - 1 + n = \frac{5}{2} + 21 - 1 = 22.5$.

Then we consider the hole: $22.5 - 1 = 21.5$.

Method 2:

By Pick's Theorem (with the holes), A, the area of a polygon is $A = \frac{B}{2} + I - 1 + n$.

B is the number of lattice points on the boundary and I is the number of lattice points inside the polygon, not touching any of the sides. n is the number of holes inside the polygon.

In this case, the area is $A = \frac{B}{2} + I - 1 + n = \frac{9}{2} + 17 - 1 + 1 = 21.5$.

15. Solution: (C).
As shown, the number of tiles is each figure below:

American Math Competition 8 Practice   Test 5

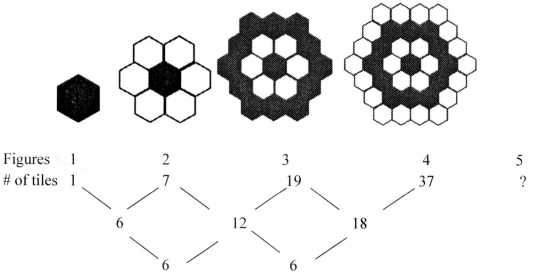

So we see the common difference is 6. Then we can get the total number of tiles in figure 5 as follows:

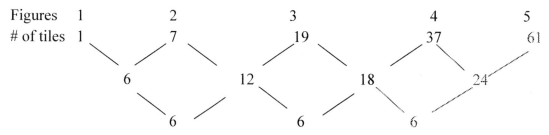

The number of black tiles needed is $61 - 37 = 24$.

16. Solution: (C). $\dfrac{37}{112}$.

We use the "C-V-S" method: C is the concentration or the strength of the solution. V is the volume of the solution. S is the substance of the solution.

Name	C	×	V	=	S
A	2/7	×	1120	=	(2/7) × 1120 = 320
			+		+
B	3/8	×	1120	=	(3/8) × 1120 = 420
			‖		‖
Mixture	x	×	2240	=	$2240x$

$$320 + 420 = 2240x \quad \Rightarrow \quad x = \frac{740}{2240} = \frac{37}{112}.$$

17. Solution: (D).
Method 1:
We distribute 10 pencils to 5 people evenly so each gets two.
Now we have 2 pencils left.
$2 = 2 + 0 + 0 + 0 + 0$. This way we have $\frac{5!}{1! \times 4!} = 5$ ways to distribute these two pencils.
$2 = 1 + 1 + 0 + 0 + 0$. This way we have $\frac{5!}{2! \times 3!} = 10$ ways to distribute these two pencils.
Total we have $10 + 5 = 15$ ways.

Method 2:
We distribute 10 pencils to 5 people evenly so each gets two. Now we have 2 pencils left. This is the nonnegative integer solutions to the equation: $a + b + c + d + e = 2$.
The solution is $\binom{2+5-1}{5-1} = \binom{6}{4} = \binom{6}{2} = \frac{6 \times 5}{2} = 15$.

18. Solution: (A).
Ben must hit 1 and 3.
Cindy: $8 = 2 + 6 = \cancel{1+7} = \cancel{3+5}$
Ellen: $18 = 10 + 8$ (only way)
Dave: $13 = \cancel{10+3} = \cancel{5+8} = 4 + 9 = \cancel{6+7}$
Alice: $12 = \cancel{10+2} = \cancel{9+3} = \cancel{8+4} = 7 + 5$
Alice hits the 7.

19. Solution: (B).
The smallest whole number that is evenly divided by each of 4, 5, 6, and 7 is LCM{4, 5, 6, 7} = $4 \times 3 \times 5 \times 7 = 420$. So the smallest whole number greater than 2 that leaves a remainder of 3 when divided by each of 4, 5, 6 and 7 is 423.

20. Solution: (D).

American Math Competition 8 Practice   **Test 5**

Because the 16 empty chairs are 4/11 of the chairs in the room, there are (11/4) × 16 = 44 chairs in all. The number of seated people is (7/11) × 44 = 28, and this is (4/9) of the people present. It follows that there are (9/4) × 28 = 63 people in the room.

21. Solution: (D).
To get an odd sum, the result of both spins must be different.

Spinner 1	Spinner 2	
Even	Odd	$P_1 = \dfrac{2}{4} \times \dfrac{2}{3} = \dfrac{2}{6}$
Odd	Even	$P_2 = \dfrac{2}{4} \times \dfrac{1}{3} = \dfrac{1}{6}$

The answer is $P = P_1 + P_2 = \dfrac{2}{6} + \dfrac{1}{6} = \dfrac{3}{6} = \dfrac{1}{2}$.

22. Solution: (B).
Because 4/11 of all the women in the room are single, there are 4 single women for every 7 married women in the room. Each married woman has a husband. So there are 7 couples. The the number of babies is 14. The fraction is 14/(14 + 14 + 4) = 7/16.

23. Solution: (D).
The distance increases as Tim moves from *A* to *D*, and continues at perhaps a different rate as she moves from *D* to *C*. The greatest distance from home will occur at *C*. The distance decreases as she runs from *C* to *B* and continues at perhaps a different rate as she moves from *B* to *A*. Graph *D* shows these changes.

24. Solution: (C).
The figure is labeled as follows. We connect *BD* and we know that *DB//GE*. So the area of triangle *GHD* is the same as the area of triangle *BEH*.

The area of the shaded region, triangle *EDG,* is the same as the area of triangle *BEG*, which is 20 × 20 ÷ 2 = 200 cm^2.

25. Solution: (D).

The overlap of the two squares is a smaller square with side length 10. The diameter of the circle has length $d = 10\sqrt{2}$ and the radius is $r = 5\sqrt{2}$. The area of the circle is 50π.

Let the area of the triangle be c, the area of the half circle be b, and the shaded area be a.

$$a = 20^2 - \frac{10 \times 10}{2} - b \quad \Rightarrow \quad 2a = 2 \times 20^2 - 2 \times \frac{10 \times 10}{2} - 2b$$

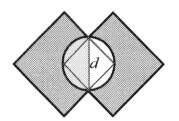

$2b$ is the area of the circle which is 50π.

So the answer is $2a = 800 - 100 - 50\pi = 700 - 50\pi$.

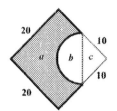

American Mathematics Competitions

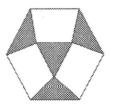

Practice 6
AMC 8
(American Mathematics Contest 8)

INSTRUCTIONS

1. DO NOT OPEN THIS BOOKLET UNTIL YOUR PROCTOR TELLS YOU.

2. This is a twenty-five question multiple choice test. Each question is followed by answers marked A, B, C, D and E. Only one of these is correct.

3. Mark your answer to each problem on the AMC 8 Answer Form with a #2 pencil. Check the blackened circles for accuracy and erase errors and stray marks completely. Only answers properly marked on the answer form will be graded.

4. There is no penalty for guessing. Your score on this test is the number of correct answers.

5. No aids are permitted other than scratch paper, graph paper, rulers, and erasers. No problems on the test will require the use of a calculator.

6. Figures are not necessarily drawn to scale.

7. Before beginning the test, your proctor will ask you to record certain information on the answer form.

8. When your proctor gives the signal, begin working on the problems. You will have 40 minutes to complete the test.

9. When you finish the exam, *sign your name* in the space provided on the Answer

American Math Competition 8 Practice — Test 6

1. Find the maximum number of intersection points in a diagram with two circles of unequal diameter and two straight lines.
(A) 8 (B) 9 (C) 10 (D) 11 (E) 12

2. How many different combinations of $3 bills and $4 bills can be used to make a total of $25? Order does not matter in this problem.
(A) 2 (B) 3 (C) 4 (D) 5 (E) 6

3. Find the smallest possible average of five distinct positive odd integers.
(A) 4 (B) 3 (C) 5 (D) 6 (E) 7

4. The number 2112 is a palindrome (a number that reads the same from left to right as it does from right to left). What is the sum of all two middle digits of palindromes greater than 2000 and less than 3000?
(A) 450 (B) 90 (C) 99 (D) 16 (E) 25

5. Cathy was born on Saturday, November 10, 2012. On what day of the week will Cathy be 776 days old?
(A) Monday (B) Wednesday (C) Friday (D) Saturday (E) Sunday

6. A birdbath is designed such that water flows in at the rate of 20 milliliters per minute and drains at the rate of 18 milliliters per minute when the birdbath is not full and water flows in at the rate of 18 milliliters per minute and drains at the rate of 20 milliliters per minute once the birdbath is full. One of these graphs shows the volume of water in the birdbath during some time interval. Which one is it?

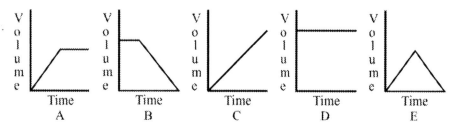

7. The students in Mrs. Lee's club were asked to do a taste test of five kinds of candy. Each student chose one kind of candy. A bar graph of their preferences is shown. What percent of her club chose candy B?
(A) 25   (B) 22   (C) 35   (D) 26   (E) 32

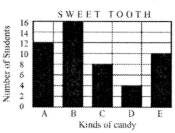

Problems 8, 9 and 10 use the data found in the accompanying paragraph and table.
Juan organizes the stamps in his collection by country and by the decade in which they were issued. The prices he paid for them at a stamp shop were: Brazil and France, 6¢ each, Peru 4¢ each, and Spain 5¢ each. (Brazil and Peru are South American countries and France and Spain are in Europe.)

Number of Stamps by Decade

Country	'50s	'60s	'70s	'80s
Brazil	8	7	24	16
France	16	8	24	30
Peru	12	8	12	20
Spain	6	18	26	18

Juan's Stamp Collection

8. How many of his South American stamps were issued in the '80s?

(A) 9   (B) 15   (C) 18   (D) 36   (E) 42

9. His European stamps issued before the '70s cost him
(A) $0.40   (B) $1.06   (C) $1.80   (D) $2.38   (E) $2.64

10. The average price of his '70s stamps is closest to
(A) 3.5¢   (B) 4¢   (C) 4.5¢   (D) 5¢   (E) 5.5¢

11. A sequence of squares is made of identical square tiles. The edge of each square is one tile length longer than the edge of the previous square. The first four squares are shown. How many more tiles does the seventeenth square require than the sixteenth?
(A) 31   (B) 32   (C) 33   (D) 34   (E) 35

12. A board game spinner is divided into four regions labeled *A, B, C* and *D*. The probability of the arrow stopping on region *A* is 1/3, on region *B* is 1/4, and on region *C* is 2/7. The probability of the arrow stopping on region *D* is

(A) 23/84   (B) 11/84   (C) 1/3   (D) 4/7   (E) 2/5

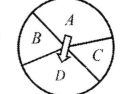

13. For his birthday, Ben gets a box that holds 216 jellybeans when filled to capacity. A few weeks later, Carrie gets a larger box full of jellybeans. Her box is three times the dimensions of Ben's. Approximately, how many jellybeans did Carrie get?
(A) 2500   (B) 5000   (C) 6250   (D) 7500   (E) 5832

14. A merchant offers a large group of items at 40% off. Later, the merchant takes 30% off these sale prices and claims that the final price of these items is 70% off the original price. The total discount is
(A) 70%   (B) 58%   (C) 55%   (D) 56%   (E) 60%

15. Which of the following polygons has the smallest area?
(A) A   (B) B   (C) C   (D) D   (E) E

A   B   C   D   E

16. Regular hexagons are constructed on the sides of a 3-4-5 right triangle, as shown. A capital letter represents the area of each hexagon. Which one of the following is true?
(A) $X + Z = W + Y$ (B) $W + X = Z$ (C) $3X + 4Y = 5Z$
(D) $X + W = 1(Y + Z)$ (E) $X + Y = Z$

American Math Competition 8 Practice   Test 6

17. In a mathematics contest with ten problems, a student gains 5 points for a correct answer and loses 1 point for an incorrect answer. If Olivia answered every problem and her score was 38, how many incorrect answers did she have?
(A) 6   (B) 5   (C) 2   (D) 3   (E) 1

18. Gage skated 1 hr 5 min each day for 6 days and 1 hr 25 min each day for 4 days. How long would he have to skate the 11th day in order to average 81 minutes of skating each day for the entire time?
(A) 2 hr   (B) 1 hr 11 min   (C) 2 hr 21 min   (D) 1 hr 31 min   (E) 2 hr 41 min

19. How many four-digit positive integers contain exactly one 0?
(A) 1972   (B) 1990   (C) 1944   (D) 2187   (E) 2016

20. The area of isosceles triangle XYZ is 18 square inches. Points A and B are on sides XY and XZ, respectively. XC is the altitude. If $XA = XB = \frac{1}{3}XY$, find the area (in square inches) of the shaded region.
(A) 11   (B) 10   (C) 12   (D) 8   (E) 6

21. Harold tosses a nickel six times. The probability that he gets at least as many tails as heads is
(A) $\frac{17}{32}$ (B) $\frac{23}{64}$ (C) $\frac{9}{16}$ (D) $\frac{11}{64}$ (E) $\frac{21}{32}$

22. Eight cubes, each an inch on an edge, are fastened together, as shown. Find the total surface area in square inches. Include the top, bottom and sides.
(A) 38   (B) 24   (C) 34   (D) 30   (E) 36

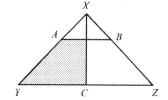

23. A corner of a tiled floor is shown. If the entire floor is tiled in this way and each of the four corners looks like this one, then what fraction of the tiled floor is made of white tiles?

(A) 4/9   (B) 5/9   (C) 1/2   (D) 3/5   (E) 4/5

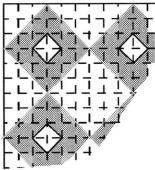

24. Mark has 100 oranges of the same size, 100 apples of the same size, and 100 pears of the same size. Mark uses his juicer to extract 10 ounces of pear juice from 9 pears, and 11 ounces of orange juice from 6 oranges, and 12 ounces of apple juice from 8 apples. He makes a pear-orange- apple juice blend from an equal number of pears, apples, and oranges. What fractional part of the blend is pear juice?

(A) $\dfrac{10}{77}$ (B) $\dfrac{1}{4}$ (C) $\dfrac{30}{77}$ (D) $\dfrac{8}{30}$ (E) $\dfrac{3}{5}$

25. Alex, Bob, Charles and Danny are good friends. Danny had no money, but the others did. Alex gave Danny one-fourth of his money, Bob gave Danny one-fifth of his money and Charles gave Danny one-sixth of his money. Each gave Danny the same amount of money. What fractional part of the group's money does Danny now have?

(A) $\dfrac{1}{4}$ (B) $\dfrac{1}{3}$ (C) $\dfrac{1}{5}$ (D) $\dfrac{5}{12}$ (E) $\dfrac{14}{35}$

American Math Competition 8 Practice   **Test 6**

SOLUTIONS:

1. (D) Two distinct lines can intersect in one point whereas a line can intersect a circle in two points. We get $1 + 2 \times 2 + 2 \times 2 = 9$ points. Meanwhile, two circles intersect at two points. The answer is $9 + 2 = 11$.

2. Solution: (A).
Since the total $25 is odd, there must be an odd number of $3 bills.
$3x + 4y = 25$.
$x = 1$: $3x + 4y = 25 \Rightarrow 4y = 22$ (no integer solution).
$x = 3$: $3x + 4y = 25 \Rightarrow 4y = 16 \Rightarrow y = 4$.
$x = 5$: $3x + 4y = 25 \Rightarrow 4y = 10$ (no integer solution).
$x = 7$: $3x + 4y = 25 \Rightarrow 4y = 4 \Rightarrow y = 1$.
We have two solutions.

3. Solution: (C).
The smallest average will occur when the numbers are as small as possible. The four smallest distinct positive odd integers are 1, 3, 5, 7, and 9 and their average is the middle number 5.

4. Solution: (B).
The palindromes are 2112, 2222, 2332, …2992. The sum of the two middle digits of them is $2(1 + 2 + 3 +…+ 9) = 2 \times 45 = 90$.

5. Solution: (C).
Since 776 days is 770 plus 6 days, it is 110 weeks plus 6 days. Friday is 6 days after Saturday.

6. Solution: (E) Initially, volume increases with time as shown by graphs A, C, and E. But once the birdbath is full, the volume begins to decrease as the rates switched. Only graph E shows both features.

7. Solution: (E).
There are $12 + 16 + 8 + 4 + 10 = 50$ students. Of the 50 students 16 prefer candy B and $16/50 = 0.32 = 32\%$.

American Math Competition 8 Practice Test 6

8. Solution: (D).
There are 16 Brazil stamps and 20 Peru stamps issued in the '80s. So there are 16 + 20 = 36 South American stamps listed in the table in the '80s.

9. Solution: (E).
His European stamps issued before the '70s include 16 + 8 = 24 from France that cost 24 × $0.06 = $1.44 and 6 + 18 = 24 from Spain that cost 24 × $0.05 = $1.20. Their total cost is $1.44 + $1.20 = $2.64.

10. Solution: (E) The '70s stamps cost: Brazil and France, (24 + 24)($0.06) = $2.88; Peru, 12($0.04) = $0.48; Spain, 26($0.05) = $1.30. The total is $4.66 for the 86 stamps and the average price is 466/86 ≈ 5.41 ≈ 5.5¢.

11. Solution: (C).
The number of tiles in each sequence is a square number. The number of additional tiles needed is $17^2 - 16^2 = 289 - 256 = 33$.

12. Solution: (B).
Since the sum of the three probabilities is 1, the probability of stopping on region D is
$$1 - \frac{1}{3} - \frac{1}{4} - \frac{2}{7} = \frac{84 - 28 - 21 - 24}{84} = \frac{11}{84}$$

13. Solution: (E).
Carrie's box is 3 × 3 × 3 = 27 times larger than Ben's box in the volume. So Carrie has approximately 27 × 216 = 5832 jellybeans.

14. Solution: (B).
The first discount means that the customer will pay 60% of the original price. The second discount means a selling price of 70% of the discounted price. Because 0.60(0.70) = 0.42 = 42%, the customer pays 42% of the original price and thus receives a 58% discount.

15. Solution: (D).
By Pick's Theorem, $A = I + \frac{B}{2} - 1$.

I is the number of dots inside the figure, *B* is the number of dots on the boundary and *A* is the area.

The area for figure *A*: $I + \frac{B}{2} - 1 = 0 + \frac{13}{2} - 1 = \frac{11}{2}$

The area for figure *B*: $I + \frac{B}{2} - 1 = 2 + \frac{13}{2} - 1 = \frac{15}{2}$

The area for figure *C*: $I + \frac{B}{2} - 1 = 2 + \frac{10}{2} - 1 = \frac{12}{2}$

The area for figure *D*: $I + \frac{B}{2} - 1 = 0 + \frac{11}{2} - 1 = \frac{9}{2}$

The area for figure *C*: $I + \frac{B}{2} - 1 = 1 + \frac{12}{2} - 1 = \frac{12}{2}$.

So polygon *D* has the smallest area.

16. Solution: (E).
Three regular hexagons are similar. The ratio of their areas is the same as the square of the ratio of their sides.
$X : Y : Z = 3^2 : 4^2 : 5^2$.
By the Pythagorean Theorem, we know that $3^2 + 4^2 = 5^2$.
Thus $X + Y = Z$.

17. Solution: (C).
If Olivia solved 8 correctly her score would be 40. Now she got 38. So she answered two problems wrong.

18. Solution: (E)
In 6 days, Gage skated for 6 × 65 = 390 minutes, and in 4 days he skated for 4 × 85 = 340 minutes. So, in 8 days he skated for 390 + 340 = 730 minutes. To average 81 minutes per day for 11 days he must skate 11 × 81 = 891 minutes, so he must skate 891 − 730 = 161 minutes = 2 hr 41 min the 11th day.

19. Solution: (D) Numbers with exactly one zero have the form
_ 0 _ _ , _ _ 0 _ or _ _ _ 0, where the blanks are not zeros.
There are (9 • 1 • 9 • 9) + (9 • 9 • 1 • 9) + (9 • 9 • 9 • 1) = 3 • 9^3 = 2187 such numbers.

20. Solution: (D)

Segments *AD* and *BE* are drawn perpendicular to *YZ*. Segment *HI* is drawn parallel to *AB* such that *H* is the midpoint of *AY*. Segments *HF* and *IG* are drawn perpendicular to *YZ*. $YF = FD = DC = CE = EG = GZ$. Connect *HD*, *AE*, *BD*, and *IE*. All the 18 smaller triangles are congruent. So the area of the shaded region is 8 square inches .

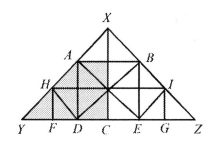

21. Solution: (E)

There are $2^6 = 64$ possible outcomes:

The following cases show that Harold get at least as many tails as heads:

TTTTTT: 1 way

TTTTTH: $\dfrac{6!}{5!} = 6$ ways

TTTTHH: $\dfrac{6!}{4! \times 2!} = \dfrac{6 \times 5}{2} = 15$ ways

TTTHHH: $\dfrac{6!}{3! \times 3!} = \dfrac{6 \times 5 \times 4}{6} = 20$ ways.

There are 42 outcomes with at least as many tails as heads.

The probability is $\dfrac{42}{64} = \dfrac{21}{32}$.

22. Solution: (C).

When viewed from the top and bottom, there are $5 \times 2 = 10$ faces exposed; from the left and right sides, there are $5 \times 2 = 10$ faces exposed and from the front and back, there are $7 \times 2 = 14$ faces exposed. The total is $10 + 10 + 14 = 34$ exposed faces.

23. Solution: (B).

The 6×6 square in the upper left-hand region is tessellated, so finding the proportion of white tiles in this region will answer the question. The top left-hand corner of this region is a 3×3 square that has $3 + 4 \times \dfrac{1}{2} = 5$

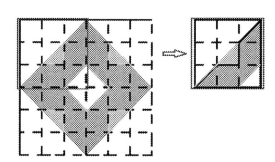

white tiles. So 5/9 of the total area will be made of white tiles.

24. Solution: (B).
The least common multiple of 6, 9, and 8 is 72.
Mark used
$9 \times 8 = 72$ pears to make $10 \times 8 = 80$ ounces pear juice.
$6 \times 12 = 72$ oranges to make $11 \times 12 = 132$ ounces orange juice.
$8 \times 9 = 72$ apples to make $12 \times 9 = 108$ ounces apple juice.

The fractional part of the pear juice of the blend is $\dfrac{80}{80+132+108} = \dfrac{80}{320} = \dfrac{1}{4}$.

25. Solution: (C).
Let A be the amount of money Alex has, B be the amount of money Bob has, and C be the amount of money Charles has.

Since each gave Danny the same amount of money, we have $\dfrac{1}{4}A = \dfrac{1}{5}B = \dfrac{1}{6}C$.

Danny's money will be $\dfrac{1}{4}A + \dfrac{1}{5}B + \dfrac{1}{6}C$.

The group's money is $A + B + C$.

The fractional part of the money:

$$\dfrac{\dfrac{1}{4}A + \dfrac{1}{5}B + \dfrac{1}{6}C}{A+B+C} = \dfrac{\dfrac{1}{4}A \times 3}{A + \dfrac{5}{4}A + \dfrac{3}{2}A} = \dfrac{\dfrac{3}{4}}{1 + \dfrac{5}{4} + \dfrac{3}{2}} = \dfrac{\dfrac{3}{4}}{\dfrac{4+5+6}{4}} = \dfrac{3}{15} = \dfrac{1}{5}.$$

American Math Competition 8 Practice — Test 7

American Mathematics Competitions

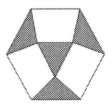

Practice 7
AMC 8
(American Mathematics Contest 8)

INSTRUCTIONS

1. DO NOT OPEN THIS BOOKLET UNTIL YOUR PROCTOR TELLS YOU.

2. This is a twenty-five question multiple choice test. Each question is followed by answers marked A, B, C, D and E. Only one of these is correct.

3. Mark your answer to each problem on the AMC 8 Answer Form with a #2 pencil. Check the blackened circles for accuracy and erase errors and stray marks completely. Only answers properly marked on the answer form will be graded.

4. There is no penalty for guessing. Your score on this test is the number of correct answers.

5. No aids are permitted other than scratch paper, graph paper, rulers, and erasers. No problems on the test will require the use of a calculator.

6. Figures are not necessarily drawn to scale.

7. Before beginning the test, your proctor will ask you to record certain information on the answer form.

8. When your proctor gives the signal, begin working on the problems. You will have 40 minutes to complete the test.

9. When you finish the exam, *sign your name* in the space provided on the Answer.

American Math Competition 8 Practice   Test 7

1. Aunt Anna is 84 years old. Caitlin is 20 years younger than Brianna, and Brianna is half as old as Aunt Anna. How old is Caitlin?
(A) 16   (B) 22   (C) 42   (D) 21   (E) 37

2. Which of these numbers is less than its reciprocal?
(A) $-\pi$ (B) -1 (C) 0   (D) 1   (E) π

3. How many whole numbers lie in the interval between $5/2$ and 10π?
(A) 20   (B) 13   (C) 14   (D) 29   (E) infinitely many

4. If a is 50% larger than c, and b is 25% larger than c, what percent is a larger than b?
(A) 10%   (B) 20%   (C) 25%   (D) 31%   (E) None of these

5. Each principal of Hope Middle School serves exactly one 4-year term. What is the maximum number of principals this school could have during a 22-year period?
(A) 6   (B) 4   (C) 7   (D) 5   (E) 8

6. Figure $ABCD$ is a square. Inside this square three smaller squares are drawn with side lengths as labeled. The area of the shaded L-shaped region is

(A) 11   (B) 10   (C) 12.5   (D) 14   (E) 15

7. Find the minimum possible product of three different numbers of the set $\{-10, -9, -7, 0, 4, 6, 11\}$.
(A) 0   (B) -660 (C) -210 (D) -630 (E) 0

American Math Competition 8 Practice Test 7

8. Four dice with faces numbered 1 through 6 are stacked as shown. Nine of the twenty four faces are visible, leaving fifteen faces hidden (back, bottom, between). The total number of dots NOT visible in this view is
(A) 31 (B) 42 (C) 54 (D) 55 (E) 52

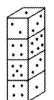

9. How many ways can the number 10 be written as the sum of exactly three positive and not necessarily different integers if the order in which the sum is written does not matter? For example, 10 = 1 + 4 + 5 is one such sum. This sum is the same as 10 = 4 + 1 + 5.
(A) 5 (B) 6 (C) 7 (D) 8 (E) 10

10. Alex and Sara were once the same height. Since then Sara has grown 50% while Alex has grown half as many inches as Sara. Sara is now 90 inches tall. How tall, in inches, is Alex now?
(A) 68 (B) 55 (C) 72 (D) 74 (E) 75

11. The number 12 has the property that it is divisible by its units digit. How many two digits positive integers have this property?
(A) 40 (B) 39 (C) 41 (D) 38 (E) 20

12. A block wall 500 feet long and 9 feet high will be constructed using blocks that are 1 foot high and either 2 feet long or 1 foot long (no blocks may be cut). The vertical joins in the blocks must be staggered as shown, and the wall must be even on the ends. What is the smallest number of blocks needed to build this wall?
(A) 2344 (B) 2347 (C) 2350 (D) 2253 (E) 2356

13. In triangle CAT, we have $\angle ACT = \angle ATC$ and $\angle CAT = 30°$. If TR and TS trisects $\angle ATC$, find $\angle CTS$.
(A) 54° (B) 108° (C) 50° (D) 30° (E) 100°

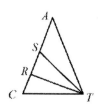

14. What is the units digit of $2013^{2013} + 2014^{2014}$?
(A) 0 (B) 1 (C) 2 (D) 9 (E) 8

15. Triangles *ABC, ADE,* and *EFG* are all equilateral. Points *D* and *G* are midpoints of *AC* and *AE*, respectively. If $AB = 2x$, $BC = x + 8$, find the perimeter of figure *ABCDEFG*.
(A) 48 (B) 46 (C) 60 (D) 66 (E) 42

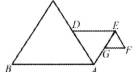

16. In order for Matt to walk 6 kilometer in his rectangular backyard, he must walk the length 75 times or walk its perimeter 25 times. What is the area of Matt's backyard in square meters?
(A) 2400 (B) 3000 (C) 3200 (D) 4000 (E) 1000

17. We define the operation "⊗" as follows: $a \otimes b = a \times b + a - b$. What is the value of the expression $(3 \otimes 5) \otimes (5 \otimes 3)$?
(A) 217 (B) 213 (C) 117 (D) 169 (E) None of these

18. Consider these two geoboard quadrilaterals. Which of the following statements is true?

(A). The area of quadrilateral I is more than the area of quadrilateral II.

(B). The area of quadrilateral I is less than the area of quadrilateral II.

(C). The quadrilaterals have the same area and the same perimeter.

(D). The quadrilaterals have the same area, but the perimeter of I is more than the perimeter of II.

(E). The quadrilaterals have the same area, but the perimeter of I is less than the perimeter of II.

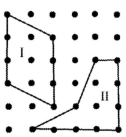

19. Three circular arcs of radius 10 units bound the region shown. Arcs *AB* and *AD* are quarter-circles, and arc *BCD* is a semicircle. What is the area, in square units, of the shaded region?

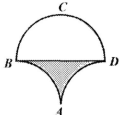

(A) $100 - 25\pi$ (B) $100 - 50\pi$ (C) $200 - 50\pi$
(D) 200 (E) 50π

20. You have a collection of pennies, nickels, dimes, and quarters having a total value of $1.02, with at least one coin of each type. What is the least possible number of coins if the total number of coins is greater than 8?
(A) 9 (B) 8 (C) 7 (D) 10 (E) 11

21. Keith tosses two pennies and Evan tosses three pennies. The probability that Evan gets the same number of heads that Keith gets is

(A) $\dfrac{1}{6}$ (B) $\dfrac{5}{16}$ (C) $\dfrac{5}{7}$ (D) $\dfrac{7}{16}$ (E) $\dfrac{3}{7}$

22. A cube has edge length 5. Suppose that we glue a cube of edge length 1 in the center of each face of the big cube. The percent increase in the surface area (sides, top, and bottom) from the original cube to the new solid formed is closest to:
(A) 25 (B) 20 (C) 16 (D) 21 (E) 10

23. There is a list of seventeen numbers. The average of the first eight numbers is 43, and the average of the last eight numbers is 57. If the average of all seventeen numbers is $60\dfrac{4}{17}$, then the 9th number is
(A) 225 (B) 224 (C) 226 (D) 27 (E) 37.

24. As shown in the figure, if ∠B + ∠D = 75°, find ∠A + ∠AGF.
(A) 106°   (B) 60°   (C) 120°   (D) 105°   (E) 90°

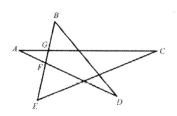

25. The area of rectangle ABCD is 144. E is a point on BC and F is a point on CD. BE = 2EC. CF = 2DF. Find the area of that triangle AEF.
(A) 42   (B) 56   (C) 60   (D) 36   (E) 40

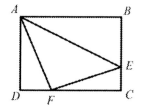

SOLUTIONS:

1. Solution: (B).
Brianna is half as old as Aunt Anna, so Brianna is 42 years old. Caitlin is 20 years younger than Brianna, so Caitlin is 22 years old.

2. Solution: (A).
The number 0 has no reciprocal, and 1 and −1 are their own reciprocals. This leaves only π and $-\pi$. The reciprocal of π is $1/\pi$, but π is greater than $1/\pi$. The reciprocal of $-\pi$ is $-1/\pi$, and $-\pi$ is less than $-1/\pi$.

3. Solution: (D).
$5/2 = 2.5$. So the smallest whole number in the interval is 3. $10 \times 3.14 = 31.4$. So the largest whole number in the interval is 31. There are $31 - 3 + 1 = 29$ whole numbers in the interval.

4. Solution: (B).
$a = 1.5c$ \hfill (1)
$b = 1.25c$ \hfill (2)
(1) ÷ (2): $a = 1.2b$.
So a is 20% larger than b.

5. Solution: (C).
If the first year of the 22-year period was the final year of a principal's term, then in the next 20 years 5 more principals would serve, and the last year of the period would be the first year of the seventh principal's term.
Therefore, the maximum number of principals who can serve during a 22-year period is 7.

6. Solution: (A).
The L-shaped region is made up of two rectangles with area $5 \times 1 = 5$ plus the corner square with area $1 \times 1 = 1$, so the area of the L-shaped figure is $2 \times 5 + 1 = 11$.

7. Solution: (B).
Since we want to find the smallest product, we need the negative value. The only way to get a negative product using three numbers is to multiply one negative number and two positives or three negatives. Only two reasonable choices exist: $(-10) \times (-9) \times (-7) = -630$, and $(-10) \times (6) \times (11) = -660$.
The latter is smaller.

8. Solution: (D).
The numbers on one die total $1 + 2 + 3 + 4 + 5 + 6 = 21$, so the numbers on the four dice total 84. Numbers 1, 1, 2, 3, 3, 4, 4, 5, 6 are visible, and these total 29. This leaves $84 - 29 = 55$ not seen.

9. Solution: (D).
$10 = 8 + 1 + 1 = 7 + 2 + 1 = 6 + 3 + 1 = 6 + 2 + 2 = 5 + 4 + 1 = 5 + 3 + 2 = 4 + 4 + 2 = 4 + 3 + 3$.
Total 8 ways.

10. Solution: (E).
Sara is 90 inches tall. This is 1.5 times the common starting height, so the starting height was $90/1.5 = 60$ inches. Sara has grown $90 - 60 = 30$ inches. Therefore, Alex grew 15 inches and is now 75 inches tall.

11. Solution: (C).
Twenty seven numbers ending with 1, 2, or 5 have this property.
They are 11, 21, 31, 41, 51, 61, 71, 81, 91; 12, 22, 32, 42, 52, 62, 72, 82, 92; 15, 25, 35, 45, 55, 65, 75, 85, 95.
In addition, we have 33, 63, 93; 24, 44, 64, 84; 36, 66, 96; 77; 48, 88; 99.
Total: $27 + 3 + 4 + 3 + 1 + 2 + 1 = 41$.

12. Solution: (D).
If the vertical joins were not staggered, each row of the wall could be built with ($500/2 = 250$ of the two-foot blocks. To stagger the joins, we need $500/2 - 1 + 2 = 251$ blocks (one of the longer blocks is replaced by two shorter ones, placing one at each end).
So the number of blocks is $250 \times 6 + 251 \times 3 = 2253$.

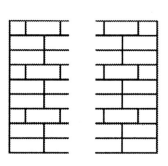

American Math Competition 8 Practice   Test 7

13. Solution: (C).
Since $\angle ACT = \angle ATC$ and $\angle CAT = 30°$, we have $2(\angle ATC) = 180° - 30° = 150°$ and $\angle ATC = 75°$. Because TR and TS trisects $\angle ATC$, $\angle CTS = \frac{2}{3} \times \angle ACT = \frac{2}{3} \times 75° = 50°$.

14. Solution: (D).
The units digit of 2013^{2013} is the same as the units digit of 3^{2013} and the units digit of 2014^{2014} is the same as the units digit of 4^{2014}.
Note that

n	1	2	3	4	Period
3^n	3	9	7	1	4
4^n	4	6			2

So the units digit of 3^{2013} is the same as the units digit of $3^{4 \times 503 + 1}$ (which is 3) and the units digit of 4^{2014} is the same as the units digit of 4^2 (which is 6).
So the answer is $3 + 6 = 9$.

15. Solution: (C).
We have $2x = x + 8 \Rightarrow x = 8$.
$AB + BC + CD + DE + EF + FG + GA = 16 + 16 + 8 + 8 + 4 + 4 + 4 = 60$.

16. Solution: (C).
The perimeter is $25 \times P = 6000 \Rightarrow P = 240$.
The length of the backyard is $75 \times L = 8 \Rightarrow L = 80$.
$2(L + W) = P \Rightarrow 2(80 + W) = 240 \Rightarrow W = 40$.
The area is $80 \times 40 = 3200$.

17. Solution: (A).
$3 \otimes 5 = 3 \times 5 + 3 - 5 = 13$.
$5 \otimes 3 = 5 \times 3 + 5 - 3 = 17$.
$13 \otimes 17 = 13 \times 17 + 13 - 17 = 217$.

18. Solution: (E).

By the Pick's law, the area I: $\frac{8}{2}+3-1=6$ and the area of II: $\frac{10}{2}+2-1=6$. So they have the same area.

The perimeter for I: $3 + 3 + 2x$.
The perimeter for II: $3 + 4 + 2x + 1$.
So the perimeter of I is less than the perimeter of II.
E is the correct answer.

19. Solution: (C).
Method 1:
We draw four circles as shown. The desired area will be
[The area of the square – the area of the circle (two half circles)] ÷ 2.
So the answer is $[20 \times 20 - \pi \times (10)^2] \div 2 = 200 - 50\pi$.

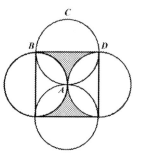

Method 2:
We create a rectangle as shown. The area of the shaded region will be
The area of the rectangle – two quarter-circles (half circle)
$= 20 \times 10 - \pi \times (10)^2/2 = 200 - 50\pi$.

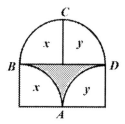

20. Solution: (A).
$p + 5n + 10d + 25q = 102$ \hfill (1)

Since we want to find the least number of coins, q should be as big as possible. So $q = 3$.
(1) becomes: $p + 5n + 10d = 27$ \hfill (2)

Similarly we let $d = 2$. (2) becomes: $p + 5n = 7$ \hfill (3)
$n = 1$ and $p = 2$.

The number of coins is $3 + 2 + 1 + 2 = 8$.

Since the total number of coins is greater than 8, this combination does not work.

We try $d = 1$.
(2) becomes: $p + 5n = 17$ \hfill (4)

We set $n = 3$ and $p = 2$ in (4).
The number of coins is $3 + 1 + 2 + 3 = 9$.
The solution is 9: 3 quarters, 1 dime, 3 nickels, and 2 pennies.

21. Solution: (B).
Outcomes: for Keith: TT, HH, TH, HT; for Evan: TTT, HHH, THH, HTH, HHT, TTH, HTH, HHT.

Case I: Keith gets 0 head (TT) and Evan gets 0 head (TTT).
Keith has $\frac{1}{4}$ chance to get TT and Evan has $\frac{1}{8}$ chance to get TTT.
$$P_1 = \frac{1}{4} \times \frac{1}{8} = \frac{1}{32}$$
Case II: Keith gets 1 head (HT, TH) and Evan gets 1 head (TTH, THT, and HTT).
$$P_2 = \frac{1}{4} \times \frac{3}{8} \times 2 = \frac{6}{32}$$

Case III: Keith gets 2 heads (HH) and Evan gets 2 heads (THH, HTH, HHT).
$$P_2 = \frac{1}{4} \times \frac{3}{8} = \frac{3}{32}$$
So the probability is $P = P_1 + P_2 + P_3 = \frac{1}{32} + \frac{6}{32} + \frac{3}{32} = \frac{10}{32} = \frac{5}{16}$.

22. Solution: (C).
The area of each face of the larger cube is $5 \times 5 = 25$. There are six faces of the cube, so its surface area is $6 \times 25 = 150$. When we add the smaller cube, we decrease the original surface area by 1, but we add $5 \times 1^2 = 5$ units of area (1 unit for each of the five unglued faces of the smaller cube). Total increase will be $5 \times 4 = 24$.

$150 + 24 = 174$. $174/150 = 1.16 = 116\%$. The increase is 16%.

23. Solution: (B).
$$a_1 + a_2 + \cdots + a_8 = 43 \times 8 \qquad (1)$$
$$a_{10} + a_{11} + \cdots + a_{17} = 57 \times 8 \qquad (2)$$
$$a_1 + a_2 + \cdots + a_{17} = 60\frac{4}{17} \qquad (3)$$

$(3) - [(1) + (2)]$:
$$a_9 = 60\frac{4}{17} \times 17 - 57 \times 8 - 43 \times 8 = \frac{1024}{17} \times 17 - 8 \times (57 + 43) = 1024 - 800 = 224.$$

24. Solution: (D).
Method 1:
We know that
$\angle AGB = \angle A + \angle B + \angle D = \angle A + 75$ (1)
$\angle AGB = 180° - \angle AGF$ (2)
So $\angle A + 75° = 180° - \angle AGF \Rightarrow$
$\angle A + \angle AGF = 180° - 75° = 105°$

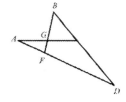

Method 2:
$\angle AFG$ is the remote exterior angle of triangle BDF. So $\angle AFG = \angle D + \angle B = 75°$.
In triangle AFG, $\angle A + \angle AGF + \angle AFG = 180° \Rightarrow$
$\angle A = 180° - \angle AFG = 180° - 75° = 105°$.

25. Solution: (B).
The area of the rectangle is $3x \times 3y = 144 \Rightarrow xy = 16$.
The area of $\triangle AEF$ = the area of the rectangle - the areas of three right triangles.

$$= 144 - (\frac{x \times 3y}{2} + \frac{2x \times y}{2} + \frac{3x \times 2y}{2})$$
$$= 144 - \frac{11xy}{2} = 144 - \frac{11 \times 16}{2} = 144 - 88 = 56.$$

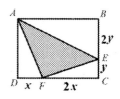

American Math Competition 8 Practice   Test 8

American Mathematics Competitions

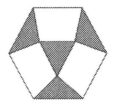

Practice 8
AMC 8
(American Mathematics Contest 8)

INSTRUCTIONS

1. DO NOT OPEN THIS BOOKLET UNTIL YOUR PROCTOR TELLS YOU.

2. This is a twenty-five question multiple choice test. Each question is followed by answers marked A, B, C, D and E. Only one of these is correct.

3. Mark your answer to each problem on the AMC 8 Answer Form with a #2 pencil. Check the blackened circles for accuracy and erase errors and stray marks completely. Only answers properly marked on the answer form will be graded.

4. There is no penalty for guessing. Your score on this test is the number of correct answers.

5. No aids are permitted other than scratch paper, graph paper, rulers, and erasers. No problems on the test will require the use of a calculator.

6. Figures are not necessarily drawn to scale.

7. Before beginning the test, your proctor will ask you to record certain information on the answer form.

8. When your proctor gives the signal, begin working on the problems. You will have 40 minutes to complete the test.

9. When you finish the exam, *sign your name* in the space provided on the Answer.

American Math Competition 8 Practice   Test 8

1. Cathy's shop class is making a golf trophy. She has to paint 600 dimples on a golf ball. If it takes him 4 seconds to paint one dimple, how many minutes will she need to do her job?
(A) 40   (B) 60   (C) 80   (D) 10   (E) 12

2. I'm thinking of two whole numbers. Their product is 132 and their sum is 23. What is the larger number?
(A) 13   (B) 14   (C) 16   (D) 12   (E) 15

3. Gary has $126. Frank has $4 more than Emily and Emily has two-third as much as Gary. How many dollars does Frank have?
(A) 70   (B) 68   (C) 79   (D) 82   (E) 88

4. The digits 2, 3, 5, 6 and 9 are each used once to form the greatest possible odd five-digit number. The digit in the tens place is
(A) 5   (B) 9   (C) 3   (D) 6   (E) 2

5. Sixteen trees are equally spaced along one side of a straight road. The distance from the first tree to the fifth is 80 feet. What is the distance in feet between the first and last trees?
(A) 90   (B) 300   (C) 305   (D) 320   (E) 240

6. James has 20% more money than Yao, and Bob has 20% less money than James. What percent less money does Bob have than Yao?
(A) 3   (B) 5   (C) 7   (D) 9   (E) 4

7. Two squares are positioned, as shown. The smaller square has side length 7 and the larger square has side length 17. The length of AB is
(A) $13\sqrt{2}$ (B) 25   (C) 26   (D) $13\sqrt{7}$ (E) 24

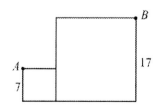

90

8. What is the probability that a randomly selected positive factor of 72 is less than 11?
(A) 1/2   (B) 7/11   (C) 2/5   (D) 3/4   (E) 7/12

9. There are 120 different five digit numbers that can be constructed by putting the digits 1, 2, 3, 4 and 5 in all possible different orders. If these numbers are placed in numerical order, from smallest to largest, what is the 73rd number in the list?
(A) 12543   (B) 23145   (C) 32415   (D) 41235   (E) 51325

10. Points *A, B, C* and *D* have these coordinates: A(3, 5), B(3, −5), C (−3, −5) and D (−3, 2). The area of quadrilateral *ABCD* is
(A) 42   (B) 55   (C) 51   (D) 60   (E) 24

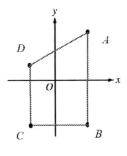

11. Of the 60 students in Robert's class, 14 prefer chocolate pie, 18 prefer apple, and 8 prefer blueberry. Half of the remaining students prefer cherry pie and half prefer lemon. For Robert's pie graph showing this data, how many degrees should she use for cherry pie?
(A) 10   (B) 20   (C) 30   (D) 60   (E) 72

12. Ted has entered a buffet line in which he chooses two different kinds of meat, three different vegetables and four desserts. If the order of food items is not important, how many different meals might he choose?

Meat: beef, chicken, pork, duck, fish
Vegetables: baked beans, corn, potatoes, tomatoes, broccoli, chives
Dessert: brownies, chocolate cake, chocolate pudding, ice cream, apricot pops
(A) 400   (B) 244   (C) 1000   (D) 800   (E) 144

13. Helen began peeling a pile of 145 potatoes at the rate of 5 potatoes per minute. Five minutes later Charles joined her and peeled at the rate of 7 potatoes per minute. When they finished, how many potatoes had Charles peeled?
(A) 70 (B) 24 (C) 32 (D) 33 (E) 60

14. These circles have the same radius. If the pattern continues, how many circles are there in the 20th figure?

    Figure 1   Figure 2   Figure 3

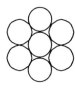
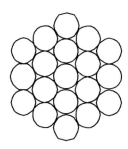

(A) 1141 (B) 1142 (C) 2000 (D) 1024 (E) 1000

15. Find a positive integer a such that $a = \sqrt{2013^2 + 2013 + 2014}$.
(A) 1002 (B) 2012 (C) 2013 (D) 2014 (E) 1007

16. Three dice are thrown. What is the probability that the product of the three numbers is a multiple of 5?
(A) $\dfrac{91}{216}$ (B) $\dfrac{125}{216}$ (C) $\dfrac{25}{216}$ (D) $\dfrac{7}{36}$ (E) $\dfrac{17}{36}$

17. How many ways can the number 10 be written as the sum of exactly three positive and not necessarily different integers if the order in which the sum is written matters? For example, $10 = 1 + 4 + 5$ is not the same as $10 = 4 + 1 + 5$.
(A) 10 (B) 16 (C) 27 (D) 36 (E) 30

18. Alex and Bob ride along a circular path whose circumference is 15 km. They start at the same time, from diametrically opposite positions. Alex goes at a constant speed of 35 km/h in the clockwise direction, while Bob goes at a constant speed of 25 km/h in the counter clockwise direction. They both cycle for 3 hours. How many times do they meet?
(A) 12 (B) 13 (C) 14 (D) 15 (E) 10

19. Four identical isosceles triangles border a square of side $8\sqrt{2}$ cm, as shown. When the four triangles are folded up they meet at a point to form a pyramid with a square base. If the height of this pyramid is 6 cm, find the area of one triangles.
(A) $8\sqrt{34}$ cm^2 (B) $4\sqrt{34}$ cm^2 (C) 98 cm^2
(D) $18\sqrt{3}$ cm^2 (E) 46 cm^2

20. There are 52 students in a class. 30 of them can swim. 35 can ride bicycle. 42 can play table tennis. At least how many students can do all three sports?
(A) 3 (B) 4 (C) 12 (D) 5 (E) 7

21. How many triangles can be formed by connecting three points of the figure?
(A) 15 (B) 20 (C) 22 (D) 25 (E) 17

22. You have enough 2¢, 3¢, and 4¢ stamps and you want to stick them in a row. How many ways are there to get a total of 10¢?
(A) 11 (B) 15 (C) 16 (D) 17 (E) 19

23. Circle B of radius 2 is rolling around a second circle A of radius 10 without slipping until it returns to its starting point. The number of revolutions the circle B makes is

(A) 3   (B) 4   (C) 8   (D) 6   (E) 7

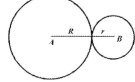

24. A box contains exactly seven marbles, four red and three white. Marbles are randomly removed one at a time without replacement until all the red marbles are drawn or all the white marbles are drawn. What is the probability that the last marble drawn is white?

(A) 3/10   (B) 2/5   (C) 1/2   (D) 4/7   (E) 7/10

25. A positive integer is randomly selected from all positive integers among 1 and 300 inclusive that are multiples of 3, 4, or 5. What is the probability that the positive integer selected is not divisible by 5?

(A) $\dfrac{2}{3}$ (B) $\dfrac{25}{37}$ (C) $\dfrac{5}{9}$ (D) $\dfrac{1}{3}$ (E) $\dfrac{4}{9}$

SOLUTIONS:

1. Solution: (A).
At 4 seconds per dimple, it takes 600 × 4 = 2400 seconds to paint them.
Since there are 60 seconds in a minute, he will need 2400 ÷ 60 = 40 minutes.

2. Solution: (D).
Since their sum is 23, only positive factors need to be considered.
Number pairs whose product is 132 are (1, 132), (2, 66), (3, 44), (4, 33), (6, 22), and (12, 11). The sum of the third pair is 23, so the numbers are 12 and 11. The larger one is 12.

3. Solution: (E).
Emily has two-third as much money as Gary, so Emily has $84.
Frank has $4 more than Emily, and $84 + $4 = $88.

4. Solution: (E).
To make the number as big as possible, the bigger digits are placed in the higher-value positions.

To make the number odd, we let 3 be the units digit. So we have 96523. The digit in the tens place is 2.

5. Solution: (B).
There are four spaces between the first tree and the fifth tree, so the distance between adjacent trees is 20 feet. There are fifteen spaces between the first and last trees. So the distance is 20 × 15 = 300 feet.

6. Solution: (E).
Let J, Y, and B be the amount of money James, Yao, and Bob have, respectively.
$J = 1.2Y$ (1)
$B = 0.8J$ (2)

Substituting (1) into (2): $B = 0.8(1.2Y) = 0.96Y$.
Thus the amount of money Bob has is $1 - 0.96 = 4\%$ less money than Yao's money.

7. Solution: (C).
Connect AB. Extend the side of the smaller square from A to C. Triangle ABC is a 10-24-26 (5-12-13) right triangle. So AB = 26.

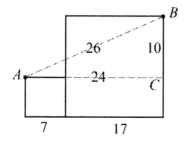

8. Solution: (E).
$72 = 2^3 \times 3^2$ has $(3 + 1)(2 + 1) = 12$ factors.
The factors less than 11 are 1, 2, 3, 4, 6, 8, and 9. There are 7 of them.
The probability is 7/12.

9. Solution: (D).
If we have 1 as the first digit, we have $4! = 24$ numbers with the first number 12345 and the last of them 15432.
If we have 2 as the first digit, we have $4! = 24$ numbers.
If we have 3 as the first digit, we have $4! = 24$ numbers with the first number 31245 and the last of them 35421.
Now we have $3 \times 24 = 71$ numbers.
The 73rd number will be 41235.

10. Solution: (C).
The figure is a trapezoid.
The area is $\dfrac{7+10}{2} \times 6 = 51$ square units.

11. Solution: (D).
Since $14 + 18 + 8 = 40$, there are $60 - 40 = 20$ children who prefer cherry or lemon pie. $20/2 = 10$.
$\dfrac{10}{60} \times 360° = 60°$.

12. Solution: (C).
There are $\binom{5}{2} = 10$ choices for the meat. $\binom{6}{3} = 20$ for vegetables, and $\binom{5}{1} = 5$ for dessert.

The answer is $10 \times 20 \times 5 = 1000$.

13. Solution: (A).
After 5 minutes Helen had peeled 25 potatoes. When Charles joined her, the combined rate of peeling was 12 potatoes per minute, so the remaining 120 potatoes required 10 minutes to peel. In these 10 minutes Charles peeled 70 potatoes.

14. Solution: (A).
Method 1:
We see the pattern for the number of circles in any figure::

Figure 1   Figure 2   Figure 3   Figure n
    1   2 + **3** + 2   3 + 4 + **5** + 4 + 3 $n + \ldots + (2n-1) + \ldots + n$

Thus in figure 20 we have
$$20 + 21 + \ldots 38 + 39 + 38 + \ldots + 21 + 20 = 2 \times \frac{(20+38) \times 19}{2} + 39 = 1141.$$

Method 2:

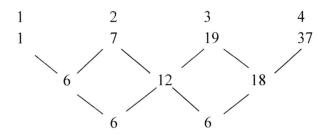

By Newton's little formula, $a_{20} = 1 + 6\binom{19}{1} + 6\binom{19}{2} = 1141$.

15. Solution: (D).
$a = \sqrt{2013^2 + 2013 + 2014} = \sqrt{2013(2013+1) + 2014} = \sqrt{2013(2014) + 2014}$
$= \sqrt{2014(2013+1)} = 2014$.

16. Solution: (A).

The probability that the product is not a multiple of 5: $\frac{5}{6} \times \frac{5}{6} \times \frac{5}{6} = \frac{125}{216}$.

The probability that the product is a multiple of 5: $P = 1 - \frac{5}{6} \times \frac{5}{6} \times \frac{5}{6} = \frac{91}{216}$.

17. Solution: (D).
Method 1:

8 + 1 + 1: $\frac{3!}{2!} = 3$ ways.

7 + 2 + 1: $3! = 6$ ways.

6 + 3 + 1: $3! = 6$ ways.

6 + 2 + 2: $\frac{3!}{2!} = 3$ ways.

5 + 4 + 1: $3! = 6$ ways.

5 + 3 + 2: $3! = 6$ ways.

4 + 4 + 2: $\frac{3!}{2!} = 3$ ways.

4 + 3 + 3: $\frac{3!}{2!} = 3$ ways.

Total 36 ways.

Method 2:
We write 10 as 10 1's. There are nine spaces between these 1's.

1 1 1 1 1 1 1 1 1 1
⎕ ⎕ ⎕ ⎕ ⎕ ⎕ ⎕ ⎕ ⎕

Any two partitions will generate a division. The partition below shows 10 = 1 + 3 + 6.

1 1 1 1 1 1 1 1 1 1
⎕   ⎕

So the answer will be $\binom{9}{2} = \frac{9 \times 8}{2} = 36$ ways.

18. Solution: (A)
Let Bob does not move at all and Alex moves at a relative speed of (35 + 25) = 60 km/h.

After 3 hours Alex has gone around the track 3 × 60/15 = 12 times, so Alex passes Bob 12 times.

19. Solution: (A).
Draw the pyramid and labeled it as shown. Draw a line
EF perpendicular to the square base. In triangle BCD, $DB = 16$. So triangle DEF is a 6-8-10 right triangle.

In triangle EDG, $EG = \sqrt{10^2 - (4\sqrt{2})^2} = \sqrt{68} = 2\sqrt{17}$

The area of the EDG is
$\dfrac{DC \times EG}{2} = \dfrac{2\sqrt{17} \times 8\sqrt{2}}{2} = 8\sqrt{34}$.

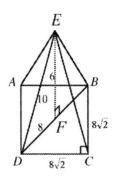
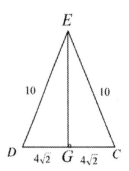

20. Solution: (A).
Method 1:
Number of students who cannot swim: 52 – 30 = 22.
Number of students who cannot ride bicycle: 52 – 35 = 17.
Number of students who cannot play tennis: 52 – 42 = 10.
At most 22 + 17 + 10 = 49 students cannot play at least one of the three activities.
At least 52 – 49 = 3 students can do all three sports.

Method 2: **The tickets method**
Step 1: Give each student a ticket for each activity he or she likes. 30 + 35 + 42 = 107 tickets are given out.

Step 2: Take away the tickets from them. Students who have 2 or more tickets will give back 2 tickets. Students who have less than 2 tickets will give back all the tickets.
Step 3: Calculate the number of tickets taken back: at most 2 × 52 = 104 tickets were taken back.
Step 4: Calculate the number of tickets that are still in the students hands.
107 – 104 = 3.

At this moment, any student who has the ticket will have only one ticket. These students are the ones who like 3 activities. The answer is 3.

21. Solution: (D).
Method 1:
We can either select 2 points from the diameter and 1 point from the circumference or select 1 point from the diameter and 2 points from the circumference

$$\binom{5}{2}\binom{2}{1}+\binom{5}{1}\binom{2}{2}=20+5=25$$

Method 2:
We use indirect way:

$$\binom{7}{3}-\binom{5}{3}=35-10=25.$$

22. Solution: (D).
We need to get N_1, N_2, N_3, and N_4.

Stairs	# of ways	Note
4	2	(2 + 2 or 4)
3	1	(3)
2	1	(2)
1	0	

With the formula $N_5 = N_3 + N_2 + N_1$, the sequence can be obtained as follows: 0, 1, 1, 2, 2, 4, 5, 8, 11, 17.

23. Solution: (D).
Let N be the number of revolutions the circle B makes.

$$N = \frac{2\pi(R+r)}{2\pi \times r} = \frac{R}{r}+1 = \frac{10}{2}+1 = 6.$$

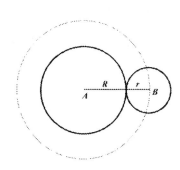

24. Solution: (D).
Think of continuing the drawing until all seven marbles are removed from the box. There are $\dfrac{7!}{4! \times 3!} = \dfrac{7 \times 6 \times 5 \times 4!}{4! \times 3!} = \dfrac{7 \times 6 \times 5}{3!} = 35$ possible orderings of the colors
Since we want that last marble drawn is white, so we avoid using all the red marbles in our arrangements (we just use 3 red marbles with 3 white marbles). There are
$\dfrac{6!}{3! \times 3!} = \dfrac{6 \times 5 \times 4 \times 3!}{3! \times 3!} = \dfrac{6 \times 5 \times 4}{3!} = 20$ arrangements.
The last marble will be white with probability $P = \dfrac{20}{35} = \dfrac{4}{7}$.

25. Solution: (A).
Let circle A represent the set of numbers divisible by 3, circle B represent the set of numbers divisible by 5, and circle C represent the set of numbers divisible by 4.

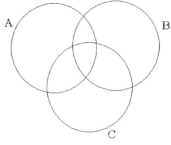

We want to find the shaded area in the figure below.

To find the shaded area, we find the union of sets A, B and C, and then subtract that from the set B to get the final result.

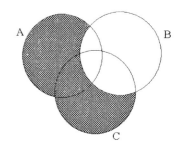

$\left\lfloor \dfrac{300}{3} \right\rfloor + \left\lfloor \dfrac{300}{4} \right\rfloor + \left\lfloor \dfrac{300}{5} \right\rfloor - \left\lfloor \dfrac{300}{3 \times 4} \right\rfloor - \left\lfloor \dfrac{300}{3 \times 5} \right\rfloor - \left\lfloor \dfrac{300}{4 \times 5} \right\rfloor + \left\lfloor \dfrac{300}{3 \times 4 \times 5} \right\rfloor$
$= 100 + 75 + 60 - 25 - 20 - 15 + 5 = 180$

$\left\lfloor \dfrac{300}{5} \right\rfloor = 60$

$180 - 60 = 120$.

The probability is $P = \dfrac{120}{180} = \dfrac{2}{3}$.

American Math Competition 8 Practice Test 9

American Mathematics Competitions

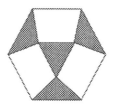

Practice 9
AMC 8
(American Mathematics Contest 8)

INSTRUCTIONS

1. DO NOT OPEN THIS BOOKLET UNTIL YOUR PROCTOR TELLS YOU.

2. This is a twenty-five question multiple choice test. Each question is followed by answers marked A, B, C, D and E. Only one of these is correct.

3. Mark your answer to each problem on the AMC 8 Answer Form with a #2 pencil. Check the blackened circles for accuracy and erase errors and stray marks completely. Only answers properly marked on the answer form will be graded.

4. There is no penalty for guessing. Your score on this test is the number of correct answers.

5. No aids are permitted other than scratch paper, graph paper, rulers, and erasers. No problems on the test will require the use of a calculator.

6. Figures are not necessarily drawn to scale.

7. Before beginning the test, your proctor will ask you to record certain information on the answer form.

8. When your proctor gives the signal, begin working on the problems. You will have 40 minutes to complete the test.

9. When you finish the exam, *sign your name* in the space provided on the Answer.

American Math Competition 8 Practice — Test 9

1. Emily plans to eat an average of 10 apples per week for 10 weeks. For the first 5 weeks she plans to eat 9 apples each week and the for next four weeks she plans to eat 8, 12, 7, and 15 apples each week, respectively. How many apples must she plan to eat during the final week to reach her goal?
(A) 9   (B) 10   (C) 11   (D) 8   (E) 13

2. Eight-hundred fifty students were surveyed about their pasta preferences. The choices were lasagna, manicotti, ravioli and spaghetti. The results of the survey are displayed in the bar graph. What is the ratio of the number of students who preferred lasagna to the number of students who preferred manicotti?
(A) 5/4   (B) 5/2   (C) 5/3   (D) 3/5   (E) 4/3

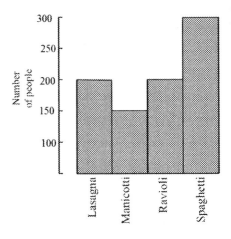

3. What is the sum of the two smallest distinct prime factors of 3232?
(A) 4   (B) 18   (C) 103   (D) 101   (E) 102

4. A haunted house has twelve windows. In how many ways can Gary the Ghost enter the house by one window and leave by a different window?
(A) 144   (B) 121   (C) 118   (D) 132   (E) 36

5. Charles wants to buy a $600 mountain bike. He has saved $200. For his birthday, his grandparents send him $150, his aunt sends him $135 and his cousin gives him $5. He earns $10 per week for his paper route. In how many weeks will he be able to buy the mountain bike?
(A) 10   (B) 11   (C) 7   (D) 8   (E) 9

American Math Competition 8 Practice — Test 9

6. The average cost of a long-distance call in the USA in 1995 was 32 cents per minute, and the average cost of a long-distance call in the USA in 2003 was 9 cents per minute. Find the approximate percent decrease in the cost per minute of a long-distance call.
(A) 23   (B) 50   (C) 60   (D) 41   (E) 80

7. The average age of 9 people in a room is 20 years. A 28-year-old person leaves the room. What is the average age of the eight remaining people?
(A) 17   (B) 16   (C) 20   (D) 19   (E) 21

8. In trapezoid ABCD, AD is perpendicular to DC, AD = AB = 5, and DC = 17. In addition, E is on DC, and BE is parallel to AD. Find the length of BC.
(A) 3   (B) 13   (C) 6   (D) 9   (E) 18

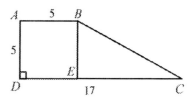

9. To complete the grid below, each of the digits 1 through 4 must occur once in each row and once in each column. What number is x?
(A) 1   (B) 2   (C) 3   (D) 4   (E) cannot be determined

10. For any positive integer n, define $\sigma(n)$ to be the sum of the positive factors of n. For example, $\sigma(6) = 1 + 2 + 3 + 6 = 12$. Find $\sigma(210)$.
(A) 471   (B) 506   (C) 534   (D) 576   (E) 471

11. Tiles I, II, III and IV are translated so one tile coincides with each of the rectangles A, B, C and D. In the final arrangement, the two numbers on any side common to two adjacent tiles must be the same. Which of the tiles is translated to Rectangle C ?
(A) I   (B) II   (C) IV   (D) III   (E) cannot be determined

12. A unit hexagram is composed of a regular hexagon of side length 1 and its 6 equilateral triangular extensions, with vertices connected as shown in the diagram. What is the ratio of the shaded area of the extensions to the area of the original hexagon?
(A) 1:1   (B) 6:5   (C) 3:2   (D) 2:1   (E) 3:1

13. The number of elements in set A is twice the number of elements in set B. As shown in the Venn diagram, their union has 2014 elements and their intersection has 497 elements. Find the number of elements in B .
(A) 503   (B) 1176   (C) 837   (D) 507   (E) 1510

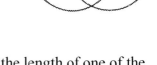

14. The base of isosceles $\triangle ABC$ is 48 and its area is 168. What is the length of one of the congruent sides?
(A) 8   (B) 15   (C) 25   (D) 17   (E) 7

15. Let a, b and c be distinct integers with $a < b < c < 0$. Which of the following is true?
(A) $a + c < b$ (B) $ab < c$ (C) $a + b > c$ (D) $ac > ab$ (E) $c = a$

American Math Competition 8 Practice — Test 9

16. Amanda draws six circles with radii 2, 4, 6, 8 10 and 12. Then for each circle she plots the point (D, A), where D is its diameter and A is its area. Which of the following could be her graph?

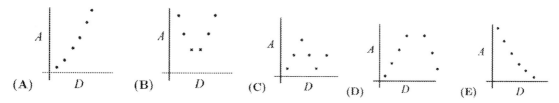

17. A mixture of 80 liters of paint is 35% yellow tint, 45% red tint and 20% water. Twenty four liters of yellow tint are added to the original mixture. What is the percent of yellow tint in the new mixture?
(A) 45   (B) 35   (C) 50   (D) 45   (E) 30

18. The product of the two 2016-digit numbers 707,070,707, . . . ,070,707 and 909,090,909, . . . ,090,909 has thousands digit A and units digit B. What is the sum of A and B?
(A) 3   (B) 5   (C) 6   (D) 8   (E) 10

19. 100 students are arranged in several rows (more than 5 rows). The numbers of students in each row are consecutive positive integers. How many students are there in the first row?
(A) 10   (B) 5   (C) 9   (D) 18   (E) 8

20. Before district play, the Unicorns had won 55% of their basketball games. During district play, they won nine more games and lost two, to finish the season having won 60% their games. How many games did the Unicorns play in all?
(A) 48   (B) 59   (C) 52   (D) 54   (E) 60

21. A bag contains 1 black ball, 3 white balls, and 4 red balls. Two balls are randomly drawn without replacement. What is the probability of selecting two balls of different colors?
(A) $\frac{1}{8}$ (B) $\frac{3}{8}$ (C) $\frac{9}{28}$ (D) $\frac{19}{28}$ (E) $\frac{5}{8}$

22. A lemming sits at *A*, a corner of a square *ABCD* with side length $10\sqrt{2}$ meters. The lemming runs 4 meters along a diagonal toward *C*, the opposite corner. It stops, makes a 90° right turn and runs 3 more meters. A scientist measures *a, b, c,* and *d*, the shortest distances between the lemming and each corner of the square, as shown. What is the average of a^2, b^2, c^2, d^2 ?
(A) 25   (B) 45   (C) 145   (D) 162   (E) 265

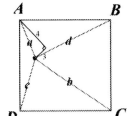

23. What is the area of the shaded pinwheel shown in the 5 × 5 grid?
(A) 4   (B) 8   (C) 6   (D) 10   (E) 12

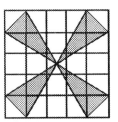

24. A bag contains six pieces of paper, each labeled with one of the digits 1, 2, 3, 4, 5 or 6, with no repeats. Three of these pieces are drawn, one at a time without replacement, to construct a three-digit number. What is the probability that the three-digit number is a multiple of 3?
(A) 1/4   (B) 1/3   (C) 2/5   (D) 2/3   (E) 4/5

25. On the dart board shown in the figure, the outer circle has radius 6 and the inner circle has radius 3. Three radii divide each circle into three congruent regions, with point values shown. The probability that a dart will hit a given region is proportional to the area of the region. When two darts hit this board, what is the probability that the sum of the two scores is even?
(A) $\frac{19}{36}$ (B) $\frac{37}{72}$ (C) $\frac{35}{72}$ (D) $\frac{1}{2}$ (E) $\frac{31}{72}$

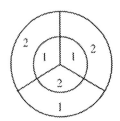

American Math Competition 8 Practice — Test 9

SOLUTIONS:

1. Solution: (E).
The first 5 weeks Emily plan to eat a total of 5 ×9 = 45 apples. For the next four weeks, she plans to eat 8 + 12 + 7 + 15 = 42 apples.
She plans to eat 10 × 10 = 100 apples. She must eat 100 − 45 − 42 = 13 apples during the final week.

2. Solution: (E) The ratio of the number of students who preferred lasagna to the number of students who preferred manicotti is 200/150 = 4/3.

3. Solution: (C).
The prime factorization of 3232 is 2 • 2 • 2 • 2 • 2 • 101. The sum of 2 and 101 is 103.

4. Solution: (D).
Gary has 12 choices for the window in which to enter. After entering, Gary has 11 choices for the window from which to exit. So altogether there are 12 × 11 = 132 different ways for Gary to enter one window and exit another.

5. Solution: (B).
For his birthday, Charles gets 200 + 150 + 135 + 5 = 490 dollars. Therefore, he needs 600 − 490 = 110 dollars more. It will take Charles 110/10 = 11 weeks to earn enough money to buy his bike.

6. Solution: (E).
The difference in the cost of a long-distance call per minute from 1985 to 2005 was 32 − 9 = 23 cents. The percent decrease is 23/32 ≈ 24/30 = 4/5 = 80/100 = 80%.

7. Solution: (D).
Originally the sum of the ages of the people in the room is 9 × 20 = 180. After the 28-year-old leaves, the sum of the ages of the remaining people is 180 − 28 = 152. So the average age of the four remaining people is 152/8 = 19 years.

8. Solution: (B).

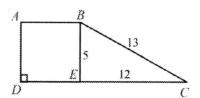

$BE = 5$ and $CE = 17 - 5 = 12$. Triangle BCE is a right triangle with the side lengths of 5, 12, and 13.

Or by Pythagorean Theorem, $BE^2 + CE^2 = BC^2$

$BC = \sqrt{BE^2 + CE^2} = \sqrt{5^2 + 12^2} = \sqrt{25 + 144} = \sqrt{169} = 13$.

9. Solution: (B).

As shown in figure 1, a must be 3 and b must be 4. c must be 3 and d must be 4.
As shown in figure 2, e must be 3 and f must be 1.
So x must 2. Figure 3 is the completed square.

1	c	2	d
2	4	e	f
a	g	h	x
b	i	j	3

Figure 1

1	3	2	4
2	4	e	f
3	g	h	x
4	i	j	3

Figure 2

1	3	2	4
2	4	3	1
3	1	4	2
4	2	1	3

Figure 3

10. Solution: (D).

Method 1:

$210 = 2 \times 3 \times 5 \times 7$. There are 16 factors: 1, 2, 3, 5, 6, 7, 10, 14, 15, 21, 30, 35, 42, 70, 105, 210. The sum is 576.

Method 2:

$\sigma(n) = (p_1^a + p_1^{a-1} + \ldots + p_1^0)((p_2^b + p_2^{b-1} + \ldots + p_2^0)\ldots(p_k^m + p_k^{m-1} + \ldots + p_k^0)$

$210 = 2 \times 3 \times 5 \times 7$

The sum of the factors equals $(2^1 + 2^0) \times (3^1 + 3^0) \times (5^1 + 5^0) \times (7^1 + 7^0) = 3 \times 4 \times 6 \times 8 = 576$.

11. Solution: (D)

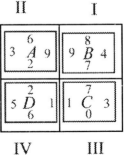

12. Solution: (A).

The original regular hexagon is cut into 6 congruent equilateral triangles. Equilateral triangle with the area y is congruent to the equilateral triangle with the area z. Isosceles triangle with the area x has the same height and same base with the triangle with the area y. So $x = z$ and $6x = 6z$.
Therefore, the ratio of the area of the shaded area to the area of the original hexagon is 1:1.

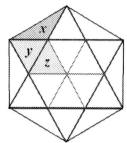

13. Solution: (C).

Let m denote the number of elements that are in A but not in B. Let n denote the number of elements that are in B but not in A.

So we have

$m + n + 497 = 2014$ $\Rightarrow$ $m + n = 1517$ (1)

$m + 497 = 2(n + 497)$ $\Rightarrow$ $m - 2n = 497$ (2)

(1) − (2): $3n = 1020$ $\Rightarrow$ $n = 340$

So the number of elements in set B is $497 + 340 = 837$.

14. Solution: (C).

Let BD be the altitude from B to AC in $\triangle ABC$.

$\dfrac{AC \times BD}{2} = 168$ $\Rightarrow$ $\dfrac{48 \times BD}{2} = 168$

$\Rightarrow$ $BD = 7$

Because $\triangle ABC$ is isosceles, BD bisects AC. $AD = DC = 24$. $\triangle ABD$ is a 7-24-25 right triangle. So the length of one of the congruent sides is 25.

15. Solution: (A).

From the number line we see that only (A) is true.

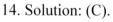

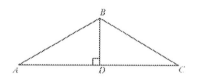

16. Solution: (A).

$A = \frac{1}{4}\pi D^2$. It represents an increasing quadratic function, called a parabola. (E) is also a graph of parabola but when D is zero, A is not zero. So (E) is excluded.

17. Solution: (C).

There are 0.35(80) = 28 liters of yellow tint in the original 80-liter mixture. After adding twenty four liters of yellow tint, 24 + 28 = 52 of the 80 + 24 = 104 liters of the new mixture are yellow tint. The percent of yellow tint in the new mixture is 100 × 52/104 = 0.5 = 50%.

18. Solution: (B).

To find A and B, it is sufficient to consider only 707 × 909, because 0 is in the thousands place in both factors.
707 × 909 = 642663.
So $A = 2$ and $B = 3$, and the sum is $A + B = 2 + 3 = 5$.

19. Solution: (C). 9.

Let m be the number of students in the first row.
$m + (m+1) + (m+2) + ... + (m+k-1) = 100$
$(2m + k - 1) \times k = 100 \times 2 = 2^3 \times 5^2$.
We know that $k > 5$, and $2m + k - 1$ and k must have different parity. We also know that $2m + k - 1 > k$, so we can only have $(2m + k - 1) \times k = 25 \times 8$
So $k = 8$ and $2m + k - 1 = 25 \Rightarrow m = 9$.

20. Solution: (B)

Let n be the number of Unicorn games before district play.
Then $0.55n + 9 = 0.6(n + 9 + 2)$.
Solving for n yields: $n = 48$.
So the total number of games is $48 + 9 + 2 = 59$.

21. Solution: (D).

Method 1:

There are $\binom{1}{1}\binom{3}{1} + \binom{1}{1}\binom{4}{1} + \binom{3}{1}\binom{4}{1} = 19$ ways to select two balls of different colors.

There are $\binom{8}{2} = 28$ ways to select 2 balls from 8 balls.

So the probability is $P = \dfrac{19}{28}$.

Method 2:

There are $\binom{3}{2} + \binom{4}{2} = 9$ ways to select two balls of the same colors.

There are $\binom{8}{2} = 28$ ways to select 2 balls from 8 balls.

So the probability is $P = 1 - \dfrac{9}{28} = \dfrac{19}{28}$.

22. Solution: (C).
We label points E and F as shown. By Pythagorean Theorem,
In right triangle AEF, $a = AE = 5$.
Extend AF to C. $AC = 10\sqrt{2} \times \sqrt{2} = 20$.
By Pythagorean Theorem, In right triangle CEF,
$b = CE = \sqrt{EF^2 + CF^2} = \sqrt{3^2 + 16^2} = \sqrt{265}$

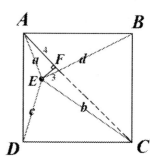

We know that $a^2 + b^2 = c^2 + d^2$. So
$$\dfrac{a^2 + b^2 + c^2 + d^2}{4} = \dfrac{2(a^2 + b^2)}{4} = \dfrac{a^2 + b^2}{2} = \dfrac{25 + 265}{2} = 145$$

23. Solution: (B).
Find the area of the unshaded portion of the 5 × 5 grid, then subtract the unshaded area from the total area of the grid.

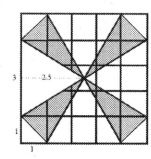

The unshaded four large triangles have the area:
$\dfrac{3 \times 2.5}{2} \times 4 = 15$.

The unshaded four small triangles have the area: $\dfrac{1 \times 1}{2} \times 4 = 2$.

So the total unshaded area is $15 + 2 = 17$.

The answer is 5 × 5 − 17 = 8 square units.

24. Solution: (C).

A number is a multiple of three when the sum of its digits is a multiple of 3.
The remainders of these numbers divided by 3 are:

Number   Remainder
1:        1
2:        2
3:        0
4:        1
5:        2
6:        0

So we see that these 3-digit numbers work:
123;   126;   153   156;   423;   426;   453;   456.
We have 3! × 8 = 5 × 8 such numbers.
The number of ways to select 3 numbers to from a 3-digit number is 6 × 5 × 4.

So the probability is $P = \dfrac{6 \times 8}{6 \times 5 \times 4} = \dfrac{2}{5}$.

25. Solution: (B).

The outer circle has area 36π and the inner circle has area 9π, making the area of the outer ring $36\pi - 9\pi = 27\pi$. So each region in the outer ring has area $27\pi/3 = 9\pi$, and each region in the inner circle has area $9\pi/3 = 3\pi$. The probability of hitting a given region in the inner circle is $3\pi/36\pi = 1/12$, and the probability of hitting a given region in the outer ring is $9\pi/36\pi = 1/4$.

For the score to be even, both numbers must be even or odd. The probability of hitting a 1 is $\dfrac{1}{4} + \dfrac{1}{12} + \dfrac{1}{12} = \dfrac{5}{12}$, and the probability of hitting a 2 is $\dfrac{1}{4} + \dfrac{1}{4} + \dfrac{1}{12} = \dfrac{7}{12}$.

Therefore, the probability of hitting (1, 1) or (2, 2) is
$\dfrac{5}{12} \times \dfrac{5}{12} + \dfrac{7}{12} \times \dfrac{7}{12} = \dfrac{74}{144} = \dfrac{37}{72}$.

American Math Competition 8 Practice   Test 10

American Mathematics Competitions

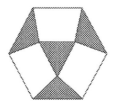

Practice 10

AMC 8

(American Mathematics Contest 8)

INSTRUCTIONS

1. DO NOT OPEN THIS BOOKLET UNTIL YOUR PROCTOR TELLS YOU.

2. This is a twenty-five question multiple choice test. Each question is followed by answers marked A, B, C, D and E. Only one of these is correct.

3. Mark your answer to each problem on the AMC 8 Answer Form with a #2 pencil. Check the blackened circles for accuracy and erase errors and stray marks completely. Only answers properly marked on the answer form will be graded.

4. There is no penalty for guessing. Your score on this test is the number of correct answers.

5. No aids are permitted other than scratch paper, graph paper, rulers, and erasers. No problems on the test will require the use of a calculator.

6. Figures are not necessarily drawn to scale.

7. Before beginning the test, your proctor will ask you to record certain information on the answer form.

8. When your proctor gives the signal, begin working on the problems. You will have 40 minutes to complete the test.

9. When you finish the exam, *sign your name* in the space provided on the Answer.

American Math Competition 8 Practice   Test 10

1. Catherine multiplies a number by 4 and gets 160 as her answer. However, she should have divided the number by 4 to get the correct answer. What is the correct answer?
   (A) 7.5   (B) 10   (C) 30   (D) 12   (E) 40

2. Mike bought fifteen folders from a store at a cost of $3.50 each. The store had a 30% off sale the following day. How much could Mike have saved on the purchase by waiting a day?
   (A) $10.00   (B) $20.00   (C) $15.75   (D) $12.75   (E) $15.00

3. What is the minimum number of small squares that must be colored black so that a line of symmetry lies on the diagonal AC of square ABCD?
   (A) 1   (B) 2   (C) 3   (D) 4   (E) 5

4. A square and a triangle have equal perimeters. The lengths of the three sides of the triangle are 6.64 cm, 8.13 cm and 9.23 cm. What is the area of the square in square centimeters?
   (A) 24   (B) 25   (C) 36   (D) 48   (E) 64

5. Soda is sold in packs of 7, 14 and 28 cans. What is the minimum number of packs needed to buy exactly 217 cans of soda?
   (A) 4   (B) 9   (C) 6   (D) 8   (E) 15

6. Suppose d is a digit. For how many values of d is $20d4 > 2014$?
   (A) 9   (B) 4   (C) 8   (D) 6   (E) 7

115

American Math Competition 8 Practice   Test 10

7. Bill walks $\frac{1}{3}$ mile south, then $\frac{5}{12}$ mile east, and finally $\frac{2}{3}$ mile south. How many miles is he, in a direct line, from his starting point?

(A) $\frac{10}{12}$ (B) $\frac{13}{12}$ (C) 1   (D) $\frac{3}{4}$ (E) $\frac{1}{2}$

8. Suppose m and n are positive even integers. Which of the following must also not be an even integer?
(A) $3mn$ (B) $3m - n$ (C) $3m^2 + 3n^2$ (D) $m + 3n$ (E) $(nm + 3)^2$

9. In quadrilateral $ABCD$, sides AB and BC both have length 16, sides CD and DA both have length 27, and the measure of angle ABC is 120°. What is the length of diagonal AC?

(A) 16   (B) 14   (C) $11\sqrt{3}$ (D) $16\sqrt{3}$ (E) $16\sqrt{2}$

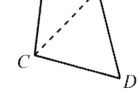

10. Peter had walked half way from home to school when he realized he was late. He ran the rest of the way to school. He ran 4 times as fast as he walked. Peter took 16 minutes to walk half way to school. How many minutes did it take Peter to get from home to school?
(A) 4   (B) 18   (C) 16   (D) 20   (E) 15

11. The sales tax rate in Belleville is 7%. During a sale at the Belleville Coat Closet, the price of a coat is discounted 30% from its $180.00 price. Two clerks, Jack and Kim, calculate the bill independently. Jack rings up $180.00 and adds 7% sales tax, then subtracts 30% from this total. Kim rings up $180.00, subtracts 30% of the price, then adds 7% of the discounted price for sales tax. What is Jack's total minus Kim's total?
(A) −$1.07   (B) −$0.53   (C) $0   (D) $0.53   (E) $1.07

12. Big A, the ape, ate 2015 bananas from July 1 through July 31. Each day he ate three more bananas than on the previous day. How many bananas did Big A eat on July 1?
(A) 20   (B) 12   (C) 15   (D) 18   (E) 17

13. The area of polygon ABCDEF is 240 with AB = 16, BC = 18 and FA = 10. What is DE + EF ?
(A) 15   (B) 16   (C) 14   (D) 10   (E) 11

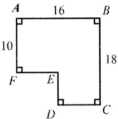

14. The Little League Basketball Conference has two divisions, with six teams in each division. Each team plays each of the other teams in its own division three times and every team in the other division five times. How many conference games are scheduled?
(A) 280   (B) 270   (C) 100   (D) 180   (E) 392

15. How many different isosceles triangles have integer side lengths and perimeter 53?
(A) 12   (B) 14   (C) 13   (D) 19   (E) 11

16. A seven-legged Martian has a drawer full of socks, each of which is red, white or blue, and there are at least seven socks of each color. The Martian pulls out one sock at a time without looking. How many socks must the Martian pull from the drawer to be certain there will be seven socks of the same color?
(A) 16   (B) 14   (C) 21   (D) 19   (E) 15

17. The results of a cross-country team's training run are graphed below. Which student has the least average speed?
(A) Angela   (B) Briana   (C) Carla   (D) Debra
(E) Evelyn

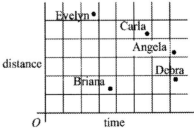

18. How many four-digit numbers are divisible by 9?
(A) 1470   (B) 1567   (C) 1000   (D) 500   (E) 577

19. What is the area of trapezoid *ABCD*?
(A) 172   (B) 188   (C) 196   (D) 200   (E) 204

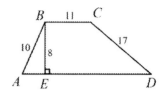

20. Two frogs Alice and Bob play a game involving a circle whose circumference is divided by 12 equally-spaced points. The points are numbered clockwise, from 1 to 12. Both start on point 12. Alice moves clockwise and Bob, counterclockwise. In a turn of the game, Alice jumps 3 points clockwise each time and Bob jumps 7 points counterclockwise each time. The game ends when they land on the same point. How many turns will this take?
(A) 6   (B) 10   (C) 8   (D) 12   (E) 24

21. How many distinct triangles can be drawn using three of the dots below as vertices?
(A) 39   (B) 12   (C) 48   (D) 40   (E) 24

22. A company sells detergent in three different sized boxes: small (S), medium (M) and large (L). The medium size costs 24% more than the small size and contains 50% less detergent than the large size. The large size contains twice as much detergent as the small size and costs 60% more than the medium size. Rank the three sizes from best to worst buy.
(A) SML   (B) LMS   (C) MSL   (D) MLS   (E) LSM

23. Isosceles right triangle *ABC* encloses a semicircle of area 8π. The circle has its center *O* on hypotenuse *AB* and is tangent to sides *AC* and *BC*. Find the shaded area.
(A) 8 − 4π.   (B) 16 − 4π.   (C) 3π   (D) 10   (E) 4π

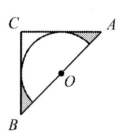

24. Figure (1) is a figure of a rectangle cutting into two triangles by its diagonal. There are 5 sides in Figure (1). Figure (2) has 16 sides, and Figure (3) has 33 sides. If the pattern continues, how many sides are in the 100th figure?

(1)

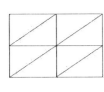
(2)

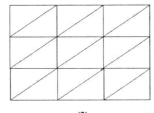
(3)

(A) 30020 (B) 30200 (C) 30000 (D) 1001 (E) 12000

25. As shown in the figure, triangle ABC is an equilateral triangle with $AB = 8$. P is a point inside the triangle such that PA, PB, and PC divide $\triangle ABC$ into three identical triangles. The points D, E and F are the midpoints of the three sides. What fraction of $\triangle ABC$ is shaded?

(A) $\dfrac{5}{24}$ (B) $\dfrac{1}{4}$ (C) $\dfrac{1}{8}$ (D) $\dfrac{2}{9}$ (E) $\dfrac{2}{7}$

SOLUTIONS:

1. Solution: (B).
If multiplying a number by 4 results in 160, then the number must be 40. If 40 is divided by 4, the correct answer is 10.

2. Solution: (C).
Method 1:
Mike spent 15 × $3.50 = $52.50 on the folders. If he had purchased the folders a day later, he would have saved 30% of this total, or 0.30 × $52.50 = $15.75.

Method 2:
Mike could have bought fifteen folders at a cost of 15 × 0.7 × 3.5 = $36.75 for the 20%-off sale, so he could have saved $52.50 - $36.75 = $15.75.

3. Solution: (D) For diagonal BD to lie on a line of symmetry in square $ABCD$, the four small squares labeled bl must be colored black.

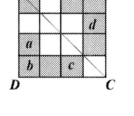

4. Solution: (C) The perimeter of the triangle is 6.64 + 8.13 + 9.23 = 24 cm. The perimeter of the square is also 24 cm. Each side of the square is 24 ÷ 4 = 6 cm. The area of the square is 6^2 = 36 square centimeters.

5. Solution: (B).
To get the minimum number of packs, purchase as many 28-packs as possible: seven 28-packs contain 196 cans, which leaves 217 − 196 = 21 cans. To get the remaining 42 cans, purchase one 14-pack and one 7-pack. The minimum number of packs is 9.

6. (Solution: C).
The number $20d4$ is greater than 2014 for $d = 2$ to 9. Therefore, there are 9 − 2 + 1 = 8 digits satisfying the inequality.

7. Solution: (B).
The diagram on the left shows the path of Bill's walk. As the diagram on the right illustrates, he could also have walked from A to B by first walking 1/3 mile south then 5/12 mile east.

By the Pythagorean Theorem,
$$AB = \sqrt{1+(\frac{5}{12})^2} = \sqrt{\frac{12^2+5^2}{12^2}} = \sqrt{\frac{13^2}{12^2}} = \frac{13}{12}$$

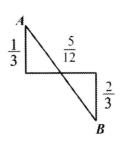
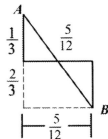

8. Solution: (E)
To check the possible answers, choose the smallest even numbers for *m* and *n*.
If $m = n = 2$, then
$3mn = 12$, $3m - n = 4$, $3m^2 + 3n^2 = 24$, $m + 3n = 8$, and $(mn + 3)^2 = 49$.

This shows that (A), (B), (C) and (D) can be even when *m* and *n* are even.

9. Solution: (D).
Draw *BE* perpendicular to *AC* at *E*.
Triangle *BCE* is a 30°-60°-90° right triangle with $BC = 16$, $BE = 8$, and $CE = 8\sqrt{3}$. So $AC = 2CE = 16\sqrt{3}$.
Or By Pythagorean Theorem, $CE = \sqrt{16^2 + 8^2} = \sqrt{192} = 8\sqrt{3}$.
$AC = 2CE = 16\sqrt{3}$.

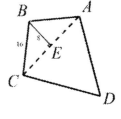

10. Solution: (D) Covering the same distance three times as fast takes one-fourth the time. So Peter ran for 4 minutes. His total time was $16 + 4 = 20$ minutes.

11. Solution: (C).
To add 7% sales tax to an item, multiply the price by 1.07. To calculate a 30% discount, multiply the price by 0.7. Because both actions require only multiplication, and because multiplication is commutative, the order of operations doesn't matter. Jack and Kim will get the same total.
Note: Jack's final computation is 0.70(1.07 × $180.00) and Kim's is 1.07(0.70 ×

$180.00). Both yield the same product, $134.82.

12. Solution: (A).
Let n be the number of bananas that Big A ate on July 1. The following equation shows his banana intake for the 31 days.

$n + (n + 1 \times 3) + (n + 2 \times 3) + \ldots + (n + 30 \times 3) = 2015$.
Or $31n + 1 \times 3 + 2 \times 3 + \ldots + 30 \times 3 = 2015 \Rightarrow 31n + 3(1 + 2 + \ldots + 30) = 2015$
$\Rightarrow 31n + \dfrac{(1+30) \times 30}{2} \times 3 = 2015 \Rightarrow 31n + 465 \times 3 = 2015 \Rightarrow 31n = 620$
$\Rightarrow n = 20$.
So Big A ate 20 bananas on July 1.

13. Solution: (C).
Method 1:
We extend FE to meet BC at G. the area $ABGF$ is $10 \times 16 = 160$.
The area of $CDFG = 8 \times DC = 240 - 160 = 80$.
So $DC = 10$ and $DE + EF = 8 + (16 - 10) = 14$.

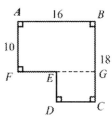

Method 2:
We extend AF and CD to meet at G.
$240 + 8 \times EF = 16 \times 18 \Rightarrow EF = 6$.
$DE + EF = 8 + 6 = 14$.

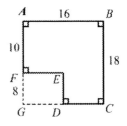

14. Solution: (B).
Method 1:
Each team plays 15 games in its own division and 30 games against teams in the other division. So each of the 12 teams plays 45 conference games. Because each game involves two teams, there are $12 \times 45/2 = 270$ games scheduled.

Method 2:
$3\dbinom{6}{2} + 3\dbinom{6}{2} + 5\dbinom{6}{1}\dbinom{6}{1} = 45 + 45 + 180 = 270$

15. Solution: (C).

Let the sides of the isosceles triangle be a, a, and c. The perimeter is 53, so we have $2a + c = 53$. $2a$ is even and 53 is odd, so we know that c is odd. We also know from the Triangle Inequality, $c < 2a$ or $2c < 53$ or $c < 26.5$.

The greatest value of c is 25.
So c is 1, 3, 5, 7…25, or all the odd natural numbers from 1 to 25. There are 13 values. For each value of c, we have one corresponding isosceles triangle, so the desired solution is 13 isosceles triangles.

16. Solution: (D).

It is possible for the Martian to pull out at most 6 red, 6 white and 6 blue socks without having a matched set. The next sock it pulls out must be red, white or blue, which gives a matched set. So the Martian must select $6 \times 3 + 1 = 19$ socks to be guaranteed a matched set of seven socks.

17. Solution: (D).

The ratio of distance to time, or average speed, is indicated by the slope of the line from the origin to each runner's point in the graph. Therefore, the line from the origin with the smallest slope will correspond to the runner with the least average speed. Because Debra's line has the smallest slope, she has the least average speed.

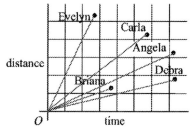

18. Solution: (C).

Method 1: The smallest four-digit number divisible by 9 is $1008 = 9 \times 112$. The greatest four-digit number divisible by 9 is $9999 = 9 \times 1111$. Therefore, there are $1111 - 112 + 1 = 1000$ four-digit numbers divisible by 9.

Method 2: $\left\lfloor \dfrac{9999}{9} \right\rfloor - \left\lfloor \dfrac{999}{9} \right\rfloor = 1111 - 111 = 1000$.

19. Solution: (A).

We draw $CF \perp AD$ at F.

By the Pythagorean Theorem, $\triangle ABE$ is a right triangle with the side lengths 6-8-10. So $AE = 6$.

By the Pythagorean Theorem, $\triangle CDF$ is a right triangle with the side lengths 8-15-17. So $FD = 15$.

So the area is $\dfrac{11+32}{2} \times 8 = 172$ square units.

20. Solution: (A).
If Bob does not move and Alice jumps $3 + 7 = 10$ points each time, Alice will be 2 points away from the starting point. With the second jump, Alice is 4 points away from the starting point. With the third jump, Alice is 6 points away from the starting point. After 6 jumps, Alice will return to the starting point, where Bob is still there. So 6 turns they will land on the same point.

The first figure shows the relative position when both move. The second figure shows the relative position when only Alice moves. They are equivalent.

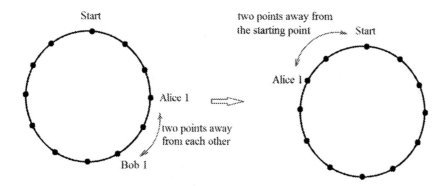

21. Solution: (C).
We have 8 points. We need 3 points to form a triangle.
The total number of triangles is
$\dbinom{8}{3} = \dfrac{8 \times 7 \times 6}{3 \times 2 \times 1} = 56$.

However, any 3 points selected from four points on the same line will not be able to form a triangle.

We have $2 \times \binom{4}{3} = 2 \times 4 = 8$ such degenerated triangle.

So the answer is 56 – 8 = 48.

22. Solution: (E).
Let V be the volume and C be the cost.
$$C_M = 1.24 C_S \tag{1}$$
$$V_M = 0.5 V_L \tag{2}$$
$$V_L = 2 V_S \tag{3}$$
$$C_L = 1.6 C_M \tag{4}$$

To determine the relative value, we compare the cost per unit weight.

(4) ÷ (2): $\dfrac{1.6 C_M}{V_M} = \dfrac{C_L}{0.5 V_L} \Rightarrow \dfrac{C_M}{V_M} = \dfrac{C_L}{1.6 \times 0.5 V_L} = 1.25 \times \dfrac{C_L}{V_L}$ (5)

So we know that the order is LM.

(1) ÷ (2): $\dfrac{C_M}{V_M} = \dfrac{1.24 C_S}{0.5 V_L}$ (6)

Substituting (3) into (6): $\dfrac{C_M}{V_M} = \dfrac{1.24 C_S}{0.5 V_L} = \dfrac{1.24 C_S}{0.5 \times 2 V_s} = 1.24 \dfrac{C_S}{V_s}$ (7)

So the value, or buy, from best to worst is large, small, and medium (LSM).

23. Solution: (B).
Method 1:
The semicircle has area 8π. So the radius is 4. Draw OD perpendicular to AC at the tangent point D. $OD = DC = DA = 4$. The area of triangle AOC is $8 \times 4/2$ = 16. The area of the quarter circle is $\dfrac{\pi r^2}{4} = 4\pi$. The shaded area is then $16 - 4\pi$.

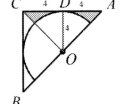

Method 2:

American Math Competition 8 Practice — Test 10

Reflect the triangle and the semicircle across the hypotenuse AB to obtain a circle inscribed in a square. The circle has area 16π. The radius of a circle 4. The side length of the square is 8 and the area of the square is 64. So the shaded area is $\dfrac{64-16\pi}{4} = 16 - 4\pi$.

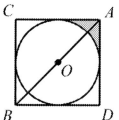

24. Solution: (B) 30200.
We see that the pattern is as follows:

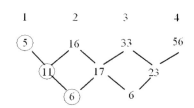

By the Newton's little formula,
$$a_{100} = 5\binom{100-1}{0} + 11\binom{100-1}{1} + 6\binom{100-1}{2}$$
$$= 5 + 1089 + 29106 = 30200$$

25. Solution: (A).
Let S be the area of a triangle. We label the areas x and y as shown.
$$x + y + x = \frac{1}{3} S_{\triangle ABC}$$

We know that $y = \dfrac{1}{3} \times S_{\triangle DEF} = \dfrac{1}{3} \times \dfrac{1}{4} S_{\triangle ABC} = \dfrac{1}{12} S_{\triangle ABC}$.

So $2x + \dfrac{1}{12} S_{\triangle ABC} = \dfrac{1}{3} S_{\triangle ABC} \Rightarrow x = \dfrac{1}{8} S_{\triangle ABC}$.

The shaded area is $x + y = \dfrac{1}{8} S_{\triangle ABC} + \dfrac{1}{12} S_{\triangle ABC} = \dfrac{5}{24} S_{\triangle ABC}$

$\Rightarrow \dfrac{x+y}{S_{\triangle ABC}} = \dfrac{5}{24}$.

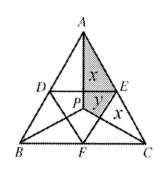

A

angle, 88, 116
arc, 81
area, 2, 6, 7, 10, 14, 16, 18, 19, 20, 21, 24, 25, 26, 27,
   31, 32, 35, 36, 37, 38, 39, 41, 42, 45, 47, 48, 51, 56,
   58, 61, 64, 65, 69, 70, 74, 75, 78, 80, 81, 82, 83, 85,
   86, 87, 88, 91, 93, 96, 99, 101, 105, 106, 107, 110,
   112, 113, 115, 117, 118, 120, 122, 124, 125, 126
arithmetic sequence, 13, 52
average, 2, 3, 4, 7, 8, 17, 21, 46, 52, 55, 60, 67, 68, 70,
   72, 73, 74, 81, 103, 104, 107, 108, 117, 123

B

base, 31, 45, 93, 99, 105, 110

C

center, 5, 12, 32, 81, 118
circle, 6, 10, 19, 20, 26, 27, 30, 31, 32, 34, 37, 48, 58,
   65, 72, 86, 94, 100, 101, 106, 107, 113, 118, 125
circumference, 42, 48, 93, 100, 118
combination, 87
concentric, 32
congruent, 2, 7, 20, 26, 47, 51, 75, 105, 107, 110
constant, 93
cube, 10, 19, 24, 25, 43, 44, 49, 50, 81, 87
cylinder, 6, 12

D

data, 68, 91
denominator, 48
diagonal, 107, 115, 116, 119, 120
diameter, 30, 31, 35, 36, 42, 48, 58, 65, 67, 100, 106
divisible, 24, 36, 79, 101, 118, 123

E

edge, 19, 68, 70, 81
equation, 63, 122
equilateral, 2, 19, 26, 29, 34, 80, 105, 110, 119
equilateral triangle, 2, 19, 26, 29, 110, 119

even number, 44
expression, 80

F

face, 19, 81, 87
factor, 19, 91
formula, 10, 12, 35, 39, 51, 97, 100, 126
fraction, 16, 21, 30, 35, 44, 48, 56, 57, 64, 71, 119
function, 110

G

graph, 1, 15, 28, 29, 40, 42, 48, 53, 58, 66, 68, 72, 77,
   89, 91, 102, 103, 106, 110, 114, 123

H

hexagon, 19, 26, 30, 34, 69, 105, 110
hypotenuse, 118, 125

I

inequality, 120
integers, 17, 19, 25, 29, 31, 42, 45, 48, 52, 55, 67, 70,
   72, 79, 92, 94, 105, 106, 116
intersection, 58, 67, 105
isosceles, 70, 93, 105, 117, 123
isosceles triangle, 70, 93, 117, 123

L

LCM, least common multiple, 23, 37, 50, 50, 52, 63,
   76
line, 2, 58, 67, 72, 91, 99, 115, 116, 120, 123, 124
line of symmetry, 115, 120
line segment, 2

M

mean, 17, 22, 29, 34
median, 17, 19, 22, 25, 29, 34, 55, 60
midpoint, 2, 45, 75
mode, 17, 22, 29, 34

American Math Competition 8 Practice — Index

N

natural number, 123
natural numbers, 123
number line, 110
numerator, 48

O

octagon, 31
odd number, 72, 121
operation, 80
ordered pair, 42
origin, 123

P

palindrome, 2, 67
parallel, 75, 104
parallelogram, 51
pentagon, 30, 34
percent, 17, 29, 30, 35, 43, 54, 68, 78, 81, 90, 104, 106, 108, 111
perimeter, 5, 10, 19, 26, 31, 42, 48, 80, 85, 86, 117, 120, 123
perpendicular, 37, 75, 99, 104, 121, 125
polygon, 61, 74, 117
power, 39
prime factorization, 108
prime number, 24, 46, 52
probability, 5, 6, 11, 12, 13, 44, 50, 57, 69, 70, 73, 75, 81, 87, 91, 92, 94, 96, 98, 101, 106, 107, 111, 112, 113
product, 4, 6, 10, 18, 24, 42, 78, 84, 90, 92, 95, 98, 106, 122
proportion, 21, 60, 75
pyramid, 93, 99
Pythagorean Theorem, 37, 74, 109, 112, 121, 123

Q

quadrilateral, 56, 80, 91, 116

R

radius, 6, 20, 37, 38, 42, 65, 81, 92, 94, 107, 125
random, 5, 6
rate, 43, 49, 64, 67, 92, 97, 116
ratio, 2, 5, 6, 7, 10, 20, 26, 27, 30, 31, 37, 74, 103, 105, 108, 110, 123
reciprocal, 78, 83
rectangle, 5, 6, 10, 13, 31, 37, 42, 48, 82, 86, 88, 119
relatively prime, 12
remainder, 18, 23, 52, 57, 63
rhombus, 2, 7
right angle, 16, 58
right triangle, 69, 88, 96, 99, 108, 112, 118, 121, 123

S

semicircle, 81, 118, 125
sequence, 39, 68, 73, 100
set, 19, 78, 87, 101, 105, 110, 123
similar, 37, 74
slope, 123
solution, 62, 63, 72, 87, 123

T

term, 52, 78, 83
total surface area, 70
trapezoid, 96, 104, 118
triangle, 7, 19, 26, 31, 34, 37, 45, 47, 51, 64, 65, 79, 82, 88, 99, 110, 115, 119, 120, 124, 125, 126

U

union, 101, 105

V

vertex, 20
volume, 6, 12, 45, 51, 62, 67, 72, 73, 125

W

whole number, 6, 37, 57, 63, 78, 83, 90
whole numbers, 6, 37, 57, 78, 83, 90

Z

zero, 7, 74, 110